# BEING
# NEW YORK,
# BEING IRISH

GLUCKSMAN
IRELAND HOUS
NEW YORK UNIVERSIT

# BEING
# NEW YORK,
# BEING IRISH

Reflections on Twenty-Five Years of Irish America
and New York University's Glucksman Ireland House

Edited by
## TERRY GOLWAY

Assistant Editor
MIRIAM NYHAN GREY

IRISH ACADEMIC PRESS

First published in 2018 by
Irish Academic Press
10 George's Street
Newbridge
Co. Kildare
Ireland
www.iap.ie

9781788550499 (Cloth)
9781788550505 (Kindle)
9781788550512 (Epub)
9781788550529 (PDF)

British Library Cataloguing in Publication Data
An entry can be found on request.

Library of Congress Cataloging in Publication Data
An entry can be found on request.

Front cover: BRIGITTE DUSSEAU/AFP/Getty Images
Design by edit+ www.stuartcoughlan.com
Set in Adobe Garamond Pro

Printed in Malta by Gutenberg Press Ltd.

Publication founded in-part by
Ireland's Department of Foreign Affairs Emigrant Support Programme.

# Contents

# From One, Many
## To Find a New Way of Belonging

—But do you know what a nation means? says John Wyse.

—Yes, says Bloom.

—What is it? says John Wyse.

—A nation? says Bloom. A nation is the same people living in the
same place.

—By God, then, says Ned, laughing, if that's so I'm a nation for
I'm

living in the same place for the past five years.

So of course everyone had the laugh at Bloom and says he,
trying to muck out of it:

—Or also living in different places.

James Joyce, *Ulysses*

# COLUM McCANN

So many skies. Over Belfast. Over Limerick. Over Ramallah. Over London. Over Paris. Over Beijing. Over Cape Town. Over Sydney. Over Brooklyn. We are a scattered people, in so many more senses than one. Our psychoses. Our passivities. Our pretensions. Our prejudices. In search of a debate over who and where we are. And where we are going. And how we are going to get there. Or if, indeed, we ever will. To be critical. To be nuanced. To understand we are as complicated as those varied skies. Not to pat ourselves too heavily on our backs. Nor to rip ourselves asunder either. To stop perpetuating ourselves from the inside. To quit being imprisoned by what they say about us on the outside. To throw our voices and tell a new story. To know that the voice comes from both within and without. To create new and sustainable moments. To reflect. To criticize. To smash the clichés embraced by the corporations, banks, government and, yes, ourselves too. To dismantle the stereotypes. To give contour to the manner to how we are seen from afar. To forge the uncreated credo. To echo. And re-echo. To be angry. To spark the smithy. To permeate the quiet corners. To chase away the craven. To sculpt a national identity that doesn't kowtow to ease. To make bridges.

To remember canals. To quit the lip-service. To be smarter than what we give ourselves credit for. To go quiet on Saint Patrick's Day. To sing late on Bloomsday. To make an Ireland of our many Irelands. To engage with what has been created. Our music. Our theater. Our painting. Our film. Our sculpture. Our literature. Our dance. All of it. The mystery of it all. To go beyond again and again. To extend past the grandiose, the narrow, the elitist. To meld and to change. To be agile. To make mistakes. To sustain the imaginative effort. To be propelled beyond the platitudes. To be properly doubtful. To do the things that don't compute. To shine the light out of the cave. To shadow-turn. To abandon destination. To embrace being lost. To practice what we have neglected. To recognize what we have ignored. To get another chance at telling. To get at the rougher edge of truth. To be raw, fierce, intelligent, joyous. To be in two places, three, four, twenty-six, thirty-two, all at once. To embrace the vagrant voices. To imagine what it means to be someone else. To learn the expansiveness of others. To accept the alternative. To create the kaleidoscopic. To crack the looking glass. To have our stories meet other stories. To be agile. To showcase our talent. To have the abandoned voices drift back in. To understand presence as opposed to absence. To demolish borders. To acknowledge the leaving. To embrace it. To allow the wound. To discover the pulse of it. To find a new way of belonging. To be also living in different places, but in diffident places too. To be everywhere. To understand that we are as much a people as we are a country. To recognize our languages. To let loose. To un-mortgage the future. To know that we cannot coordinate that which is not yet there. To stop the demolitions of what we know is good. To quit building laneways leading off into mid-air. To oppose the dismantling of enlightened social legislation. To refuse the vapid political simplicities. To end the stunned submission to greed. To shout out against the evisceration of our heritage. To make up for what we have lost. To have another chance at history. To not condescend to the past. To reimagine ourselves. To never give up on the presumption of hope.

To look out for the enquiring, lighted minds. To stand in opposition to the lobotomizing weight of expediency. To free ourselves from the small hatreds. To chant our peace. To talk principle. To sustain our self-critique. To know that what has been handed to us is precious. To weave a new flag, then wave it. To give emigrants a return. To fold the gone back into the debate. To make of ourselves an international republic. To profit for culture rather than from it. To know that there is land beyond the land. To be aware that there is territory in our imagination. To flex our muscles. To flux them. To embrace contradiction. To be joyous and critical at the same time. To shore up our commitments toward reality and justice. To be real. To be tough. To spirit on. To engage. To explore. To never forget that we have a sense of humor. To stop talking shite. And then to continue talking shite. In fact to talk more shite than anyone else. Especially when we are told not to. Then to test both theories and find an answer in each. To say then – finally – and almost – finally – well, almost finally – to reach a beginning – to never end – that we are in the continual act of composition. That there are no limits. That this, then, is our ongoing nation.

Written in celebration of the work of Loretta Brennan Glucksman and in memory of the late Lew Glucksman.

Colum McCann won a National Book Award for *Let the Great World Spin* in 2009.

# Reflections on Irish America in the Twenty-First Century

# MICHAEL D. HIGGINS

## President of Ireland

The history of the Irish in America is a long and profound one, changing with each generation. Its nineteenth-century form, for example, is rooted in dispossession, hunger and great suffering. Written into its many chapters have been many twists and new beginnings; stories of opportunity, ambition, innovation, re-invention, loss, exile and commemoration. Following the Famine of 1845–1848 it was more than reprieve. It was a location for ensuring the Famine, its causes and its consequences would not be forgotten.

Today the Irish-American story runs several generations deep, and is a multi-layered and complex one that continues to evolve and change. Across the generations that now separate us from the foundations of the Irish-American story, the community has been responding to choice.

It is a community that has matured and blended into its American landscape, now occupying a central position in the political, cultural and economic mainstream of the USA. For those who are third-, fourth-, or fifth-generation Irish Americans their Irish background may no longer dominate their American experience. Ireland is no longer a place that they call home, but they are aware of it as a distant place of origin.

For newer emigrants to the USA their experience will be one that has evolved and transitioned, now shaped and formed by the forces of globalisation. In a more interconnected world the Irish who travel to the USA do so under different circumstances from those of their forebears, and their relationship to an established Irish community has also altered in recent decades.

New technology, particularly in communications, and easier transport systems allow today's emigrants to remain strongly connected to their home country, and indeed communities, to maintain even daily contact with their families.

How, then, can we view the future of the Irish-American community as older narratives continue to fade and Irish America reaches a stage of late-generation ethnicity? The Irish community no longer connects to distinct and exclusive cultural, social and political social groups, or congregates in ethnic enclaves where their children attend the same schools, their families attend the same churches and their unique heritage remains the dominant force in their cultural lives. That community is now dispersed across the towns and suburbs of the USA, their children assimilated into a multicultural school system, their third and fourth generations identifying as American Irish, not Irish American.

For many, Ireland is now a place that is imagined, not recalled, and the bond that unites what was once a physical community is now an emotional tie maintained through the sharing of the rich heritage and culture that links them to a common past.

How, then, are we to sustain Irish-American identity in the twenty-first century? While first-generation emigrants to the USA have traditionally clustered together and sought to retain their cultural identity as a defence against what was perceived to be strange, their sons and daughters have, in their turn, been understandably determined to

Image ©NYU

assimilate into American society, embracing the culture and norms of the country into which they were born and where they were educated.

We can draw, I think, on what Pulitzer Prize-winning historian Marcus Lee Hansen has identified as the 'principle of third generation interest: what the son wishes to forget the grandson wishes to remember.' In other words, the yearning for cultural identity by a first generation of immigrants, and its rejection by their children, often returns with a third generation who experience an instinctive curiosity around the heritage and ancestry that they share with their grandparents and that connects them to the country of their forebears.

In doing so we can understand how the establishment, in 1993, of Glucksman Ireland House as the centre for Irish and Irish-American studies at NYU was a critical moment in the cultural life of both Ireland and the USA. If we are to support the ongoing existence of an Irish-American community in the USA, a community that has been and remains a great link for Ireland in political, economic and cultural terms, investment in Irish cultural programmes is critical.

Culture is based on what we share but is also a process that is continually being reworked. The work of Glucksman Ireland House acknowledges and celebrates the shared bonds of history and heritage that link Ireland and the United States, bonds that have provided a cultural interaction that has enabled the evolution of Irish culture in accordance with time, place and history. We owe so much to those scholars in the United States who, for example, recovered the social history of the late ninteenth century and our migration.

There can be no doubt that Irish culture has been greatly influenced and inspired by our wider Irish-American family, and today our music, literature and drama continues to be enriched by the interweaving of old tradition and a newer sensibility to a multicultural world.

The impact of the Irish migrant experience on Irish culture has been creative, as it has been profound and lasting. Our Irish family abroad have played a vital role in the reinvention of much of that culture; the very act of emigration itself forcing a remaking, a reimagining of the self, which breathes new life into many of our traditional art forms. Our writers, artists, directors, actors and performers have built into their craft much that is of the essence of our Irish imagination and inheritance, while creating new forms and works of art that have greatly enriched our contemporary cultural practices.

There can equally be no doubt that Ireland's traditional song, music and dance brought to the USA by generations of emigrants have not only made their distinctive contribution to the development of American culture, in particular its folk and country music, but have also created a unique and distinctive Irish-American culture that today links those in the USA who share Irish descent, connecting them to a past that has shaped and formed much of their contemporary lives.

It is that Irish and Irish-American culture that provides the rich seam holding together an evolved diaspora that has integrated into American society and are no longer the homogenous entities that they were in generations gone by. It is critical, therefore, that we ensure that newer generations of Irish Americans have access to that culture, and to an understanding of the heritage that lies at its heart.

In Ireland we are very grateful to Glucksman Ireland House, whose generous vision will reap not just academic rewards, but rich cultural and social rewards in the years to come.

Today the Irish in the USA are responsible for the continuation of a community whose foundations are grounded in the lives of those whose journeys began many generations ago. I am confident that newer generations will continue to build on those foundations, preserving an Irish-American community that blends with the landscape and skylines of America while holding, within its walls, the beat and echoes of much that has gone before.

Michael D. Higgins
Uachtarán na hÉireann/President of Ireland
6 February, 2018

# 'A Castle That Will Continue to Enhance Irish Culture and Scholarship'

# ANDREW HAMILTON
## President of New York University

Twenty-five years ago, New York University and two of the university's great friends, Lew Glucksman and Loretta Brennan Glucksman, set out to build a world-class Irish Studies program. Nobody was quite sure at the time how the process would unfold, but one thing was certain: New York City – the destination for so many Irish immigrants – offered students and faculty an unparalleled opportunity to research the history and culture of a sizeable portion of Ireland's diaspora.

And so was born NYU's Glucksman Ireland House. It began humbly enough, with a few students and two faculty members in residence, but has since grown to become a vital center for teaching, researching, interrogating, and archiving the Irish in experience in the United States. Two of my immediate predecessors, Jay Oliva and John Sexton, presided over Glucksman Ireland House's infancy and maturation, and I have been delighted to build on the legacy they created through their partnership with Lew and Loretta.

Over the years, Glucksman Ireland House has served as a stage for some of the world's best-known writers, scholars, artists, politicians, and intellectuals, including Seamus Heaney, Alice McDermott, Martin

McGuinness, Mary Robinson, Jim Dwyer, and James Galway. The House's public programs have been wildly successful in bringing the New York area's Irish community together in support of cutting-edge scholarship, brilliant literature, and fascinating performance.

More than anything else, though, NYU's Glucksman Ireland House has nurtured the curiosity and passion of thousands of students through the years. Dedicated faculty and staff, supported by an outstanding board of advisers, have placed students at the center of the mission at NYU Glucksman Ireland House. Students have formed their own organizations to foster their interest in Irish and Irish-American culture, have conducted panel discussions and conferences, and have written and published new research on an impressive array of topics.

The accomplishments of those students and their enduring interest in Ireland and Irish America speaks to the founding ideals of the program's benefactors, Lew and Loretta, and to the devotion of NYU Glucksman Ireland House faculty, staff, advisers, friends, and members. As the Irish proverb goes, *Trí na chéile a thógtar na cáisléain*, or 'In our togetherness, castles are built.' Inspired and supported by the Glucksmans, I have no doubt that we have built a castle at NYU that will continue to educate and enrich, as well as enhance Irish culture and scholarship for years to come.

Here's to the next quarter-century.

Andrew Hamilton is president of New York University.

Left:
Singer Tony Bennett and journalist Jimmy Breslin at an event in honor of Breslin's career. ©NYU.

All images ©NYU.

# Ireland

# BILLY COLLINS

My love is not like a red, red rose
in more ways than she is
like a red, red rose
or any flower in the world
of one color or another.

Right now, a red, red rose
is blooming by someone's garden wall
and I am leaning on that wall
thinking about my love,
who sleeps on a green, green island, far away.

Billy Collins served as the Poet Laureate of the United States from 2001
to 2003.

# A Door, Opened

# TERRY GOLWAY

On a fine April afternoon in 1993 they marched through Washington Square Park, dressed in the purple robes of New York University, bagpipers clearing the way, around the ponderous arch newly scrubbed of past disorder, two towers looming in the background, ever present. They proceeded across an unrushed Washington Square North toward a brick building, built for another time and for other uses, built where Fifth Avenue's addresses start and where its traffic ends.

As of this moment on April 26, 1993, that building on Fifth Avenue would be called Glucksman Ireland House.

Lew Glucksman and Loretta Brennan Glucksman, patrons of the House, founders of the feast, were at the head of the march, to the bemused delight of some of Lew's colleagues on NYU's board. Loretta would remember years later that Laurence Tisch, the board's chairman, would 'tease the daylights' out of Lew over his Irish obsession – Lew Glucksman, a Hungarian Jew, giving his name to Ireland House. They had a good many laughs over that, Loretta said. But they also knew what she knew: 'Lew,' she said, 'truly loved Ireland.'

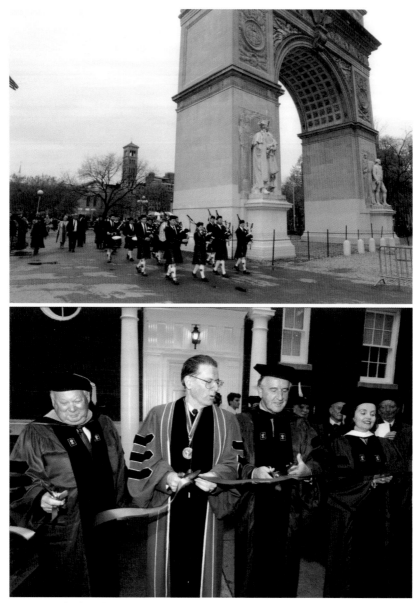

Top: Pipers leading the procession across Washington Square on opening day.

Bottom: The ribbon cutting, by Lew Glucksman, NYU President Jay Oliva, Taoiseach Albert Reynolds, and Loretta Brennan Glucksman.

The procession came to a halt outside the building, in front of a new doorway fronting the avenue. There the robed procession became a huddle of purple as the president of New York University, L. Jay Oliva, the Irish-speaking son of an immigrant from County Galway, greeted such a gathering of talent and brains and wit and personality that no round table could possibly accommodate them. Waiting to cross the untouched threshold were Seamus Heaney, with two years left to wait for his long-anticipated Nobel Prize for Literature; the Taoiseach of the Republic of Ireland, Albert Reynolds; the playwright Brian Friel; the actress Maureen O'Hara; the flutist James Galway; the producer Noel Pearson; and the humanitarian Sister Stanislaus Kennedy.

It was, Loretta would later remember, an astonishing display of Irish history, culture, art, politics … and memory. For on that glittering April afternoon in the last decade of the twentieth century there were few who did not think of those who had come before, not by air but by ship, not given the privilege of marching through the square but left to trudge through the streets of the Lower East Side and dozens of other American neighborhoods, women and men and children whose stories had not been recorded and preserved and passed on as object lessons. Had they not been who they were and had they not done what they did, there would have been no procession, no waiting on the threshold, no gathering of a generation's keenest minds.

President Oliva told the multitude that this new institution, Glucksman Ireland House, would 'provide New York City with a focal point for the breadth and depth of Irish culture, both old and new.' And then Lew and Loretta Glucksman joined Oliva in cutting a purple ribbon across the doorway and in they went, to inaugurate a space for which there were plans and ambitions and visions but which was, on this first day, very much a work in progress and one for which there was no precedent. For there was nothing quite like Glucksman Ireland House, not even in the pulsating city of a thousand identities and cultures.

Taoiseach Albert Reynolds joined Loretta Brennan Glucksman and Lew Glucksman to open the door at Glucksman Ireland House.

There were other academic houses tied to language and culture, there were other programs that focused on artifacts and history, there were other societies that sought to knit together old and new. But there was nothing designed to interrogate and narrate the history, the literature, the music, and the lived experiences of the Irish in America, all of it, in all its glory, with all its flaws.

In the days that followed the ceremonies on Fifth Avenue, New York University opened its Bobst Library for readings from Nuala Ní Dhomhnaill, Galway Kinnell, Barbara Gelb, Geraldine Fitzgerald, and a founding faculty member of Glucksman Ireland House, Denis Donoghue. Neil Jordan's film *The Miracle* was screened in Tishman Auditorium. And then, later in the week, the House's founding director, Robert Scally, delivered the first public lecture to be held in the program's new home. Scally's topic was 'Hidden Ireland.'

There was, in fact, much about Ireland and Irish America that remained hidden and unexplored in 1993, a time before Frank McCourt chronicled his childhood in Brooklyn and Limerick, before the phrase 'National Book Award winner' was attached to Alice McDermott and Colum McCann, before Jean Butler stepped on the Eurovision stage and before Terry George made a movie; before Billy Collins was a laureate and Paul Muldoon had a Pulitzer on his desk at Princeton University; before St. Patrick's Day parades in New York and Boston welcomed those who challenged old ideas of what it meant to be Irish; before a president of the United States visited Belfast and dared to speak of hope.

All of that was about to change. Glucksman Ireland House would be both a driver and beneficiary of a Celtic revival so dramatic that within three years of the ribbon-cutting on Fifth Avenue, the *New York Times* announced that the Irish were ascendant, again (which led some to wonder what they had missed the first time around). The *Times* turned to Bob Scally for an explanation of this rediscovery of Irish culture in the United States, this 'resurgence of interest in things Irish.'

'People are less defensive about being Irish now,' Scally said. 'We have lived out the old parochial ideas of what it means to be Irish.'

The space that Lew and Loretta Glucksman created – its ambition, its mission and even its geographic presence in the heart of Greenwich Village – surely was a sign of this new self-assurance among the Irish in New York. And in that spring of 1993, just a few weeks after the procession through Washington Square, another voice beckoned Irish America to open its doors, to cross new thresholds. It was the voice of the first woman to be elected President of Ireland, Mary Robinson, herself a symbol of changing times and attitudes. She traveled to New York to speak to the descendants of immigrants in the restored great hall on Ellis Island, a place ingrained in the experience of millions of Irish people at home and abroad. The president and hundreds of the New York Irish were gathered to honor the first immigrant to be questioned,

Top: Alice McDermott won the 1998 National Book Award for fiction for *Charming Billy*. ©NYU.
Bottom: Transatlantic conversation: New York's Colum McCann and Ireland's Joseph O'Connor. ©NYU.

Photo courtesy of James Higgins.

inspected, and processed on that small spit of land in the great harbor. She was a 17-year-old girl from County Cork named Annie Moore, and a hundred years after her arrival, she was immortalized in bronze, suitcase in hand, peering intently into her future as she crossed from the old to the new. The life-sized sculpture of young Annie Moore was controversial when it was proposed, for it required the authorities to reconsider what kind of people and what sort of memories deserved public recognition. They decided in favor of Annie Moore.

There ought to be more statues of people like Annie Moore, President Robinson said that night. There surely were enough already of famous men. The press reported that there was some grumbling in the audience, and one man muttered something about the Statue of Liberty just a few hundred feet away. A woman responded by saying that the list of enshrined women began and ended with Lady Liberty.

New Yorkers enjoy an Ireland House event. © NYU.

In remembering and indeed immortalizing Annie Moore, the President of Ireland and her audience were acknowledging a newly discovered piece of the transatlantic Irish experience, a narrative that New York University scholar Hasia Diner had identified a decade earlier: The typical post-Famine Irish immigrant, Diner discovered, was a young, single woman, an experience quite unlike that of any other immigrant group during the years Ellis Island was open. Annie Moore was not an exception to the Irish immigrant experience. In many ways, Annie Moore *was* the Irish immigrant experience in the late nineteenth century.

It was a profound discovery, and in the years following publication of Diner's book, *Erin's Daughters in America*, scholars would find stories that lay hidden in plain sight, stories of domestics and seamstresses and teachers lost to history and forgotten in the retelling of the great American Ellis Island story.

Economist Jeffrey Sachs and Bono. ©NYU.

Hidden Ireland. Untold stories. Forgotten histories. Unchronicled lives. These were the challenges that awaited the women and men who were about to populate Glucksman Ireland House, and they likely would not have guessed that they were embarking on a journey that would coincide with, and provide the inspiration for, a quarter-century of change and revival in Irish New York.

It surely was an unlikely journey, or so it seemed in 1993, for there were few mileposts along the way and the destination was uncertain. Irish America, one Harvard scholar would conclude, had faded into something he called mere 'whiteness,' embracing the solidarity of skin color over the cultural and religious differences, the hyphen that defined past generations cast aside in return for acceptance and assimilation. That theory received an elegant reply from the novelist and essayist Peter Quinn, who said that what was truly interesting about the Irish in America is not that they became white but that they remained Irish.

Clockwise from top left:
NYU President John Sexton greets President Michael D. Higgins of Ireland during a visit to New York. ©NYU.

Acclaimed journalist Jimmy Breslin signs a book for two of Glucksman Ireland House's most devoted patrons, Bridget and Jim Cagney. ©NYU.

Jean Kennedy Smith, a key figure in the Irish peace process during her time as U.S. Ambassador to Ireland, with Bill Whelan, composer of *Riverdance*. ©NYU.

Still, as Glucksman Ireland House announced a new era of exploration with its very presence and its ambitions, there was little to suggest that Irish America was on the verge of a cultural renaissance, that energy and vitality were hiding in the shadows of tradition and ritual. In an interview just a few years before the House opened, Senator Daniel Patrick Moynihan charted the path of Irish America since the publication of his famous essay in the landmark book, *Beyond the Melting Pot*, in

1963. 'New York used to be an Irish city,' he had written back then, and there was no accident in his use of the past tense. A generation later, he saw little reason to revise his premise, and that was not necessarily a bad thing, he said. The Irish in New York and throughout America had moved beyond the roles that had made them such a visible presence in the twentieth century – politics, journalism, labor, the Church. Now, Moynihan said in 1988, the Irish were on Wall Street and in medicine. 'And when you are a doctor,' he said, 'nobody knows your name.' And that was fine, but there was no point in wishing for a new Al Smith or a new Grace Kelly or a new Pete Hamill. The Irish had moved on – they were practicing medicine now or were managing great heaps of money, their success hidden from all but their patients and clients. Joe Lee, who succeeded Bob Scally as executive director of Glucksman Ireland House in 2002, took note of the same phenomenon, writing that 'the rise of Irish Americans to prominence in the business world' would loom large in the histories of Irish America in the late twentieth century.

As events transpired, those histories would be crowded indeed.


Dates are the bane of the reluctant student of history, and they very likely deserve the professional's scorn as well. Dates may live in infamy or in glory, but great historical change rarely reveals itself so neatly or abruptly. That said, the afternoon of September 28, 1994 surely seemed like a date of demarcation for the Irish in America, a date after which everything changed. For it was on that day that something quite unexpected unfolded on the steps of New York's City Hall as Gerry Adams, the leader of the Irish Republican Army's political organization, Sinn Fein, shook hands with the city's law-and-order mayor, Rudolph Giuliani, and heard various city officials praise him as an emissary of peace. Giuliani even hinted that President Bill Clinton ought to hold a similar ceremony for Adams in the White House, but the mayor's suggestion was seen as not just unlikely but utterly preposterous.

George Mitchell, speaking at an event sponsored by Glucksman Ireland House, served as a mediator in talks that led to the Good Friday Agreement in 1998. Photo courtesy of James Higgins.

About a month before Adams's appearance in New York, the IRA had declared a ceasefire in its decades-long campaign against Britain's presence in the six counties of Northern Ireland. The conflict inevitably had become an Irish-American issue, a presence in parades, in the arts, at academic conferences, in everyday conversation, and only a sage or a fool would venture a prediction that someday soon The Troubles would transition from journalism to history.

The ceasefire did not hold, not at first, but when weapons of war were put aside for a second time in the summer of 1997, the pace of history quickened until it burst through mildewed doors fastened by rusting bolts, once secure against change, now helpless to defend the status quo. Bill Clinton not only welcomed Gerry Adams to the White House on St. Patrick's Day, 1995, but treated him as one of several partners in a peace process that had been begun in secret years earlier, and those who were part of it – people like Irish-American publisher

Niall O'Dowd – knew to say nothing, for the whole thing was as yet as helpless as the fledglings in St. Kevin's open hand. There were hushed conversations between John Hume and men who kept their guns beside them and men who paid for those guns until the time was right and then George Mitchell crossed the Atlantic to help broker an agreement signed on Good Friday, 1997, and ratified on both sides of the island's border. Weapons were put away, handshakes exchanged, power shared, and while it was not a perfect peace it was peace all the same. And it came in the lifetime of those who thought they would never live to see it and surely they gasped or wept or simply smiled when in June 2012 the onetime commander of the IRA, Martin McGuinness, shook the hand of the longtime monarch of the United Kingdom, Queen Elizabeth II.

Historians may one day conclude that it was all coincidence, and perhaps it was, but it surely is worthy of note that hope triumphed over history in the north of Ireland at the very moment when American audiences were discovering what the *New York Times* called 'the unmistakable romance and relevance of Irish culture,' in both its native and Americanized form.

It began with a book bearing a title that sounded like so much bluster and blarney, save that the claimant was a Jesuit-trained scholar of Greek and Roman literature, of scripture, and of philosophy. Thomas Cahill told the story of Patrick, who brought Christianity to Ireland, and of the monks who later preserved tradition and knowledge when darkness fell across Europe. He called his book, *How the Irish Saved Civilization*. It sold copies by the hundreds of thousands and inspired serious reviews that could be summed up in a phrase: 'Who knew?' Hidden Ireland, steward of civilization.

After Cahill came the deluge. On stage, in print, in the local movie house – there was no escaping what Seamus Heaney would describe, tongue perhaps in cheek or perhaps not, as 'sheer, bloody genius!' *Riverdance*, already a phenomenon in Ireland after its seven-minute interval in the 1994 Eurovision contest, opened as a stage production in

Dublin in February, 1995, with Irish-Americans Jean Butler and Michael Flatley taking giant leaps with a demure art form governed by the rules of the crossroads and the parish halls. It was bloody genius indeed, paying homage to the past while breaking away from its traditions, bringing to the stage African-American tap, Spanish flamenco, Russian dervish, the music by Bill Whelan not just jigs and reels but a universal spiritual, sung by women and men from across the globe, moving from place to place, migrants knocking on doors, pleading for freedom.

The show debuted in New York's Radio City Music Hall in March, 1996, with Colin Dunne in place of Flatley, and the results were no less sensational than they were in Ireland and the United Kingdom. Tens of millions saw and heard the stage show either live or on television, indeed, they continue to see and hear it at various venues around the

Jean Butler and Michael Flatley revolutionized Irish dance and charmed the world with *Riverdance*. Butler later joined the faculty at Glucksman Ireland House. Original *Riverdance* photograph by kind permission of Abhann Productions.

world, and when the last toe is tapped and the last note sounds, they are left with an image of Ireland and Irish culture that would have been unimaginable a generation earlier.

Amid the unrestrained exuberance of early *Riverdance* came word, in October, 1995, that Seamus Heaney had won the Nobel Prize for Literature. In making the announcement, the Swedish Academy praised the poet's 'works of lyrical beauty and ethical depth, which exalt everyday miracles and the living past.' Heaney was away in Greece when the Academy broke the news, and his family in Dublin had difficulty tracking him down in that dark age of twentieth-century communication. He accepted the prize in December of that year wearing the traditional white tie and tails of a Nobel laureate, reprising the recent history of his island home, speaking with hope of poetry's power 'to remind us that we are hunters and gatherers of values.'

The Swedish Academy ratified what so many already knew: Seamus Heaney was one of the great names in world literature as the old century began to ebb. Less than a year later, a little-known retired schoolteacher in New York City published a memoir called *Angela's Ashes*, and within a week of its arrival in bookstores, Frank McCourt was transformed into a literary and cultural phenomenon. 'When I look back on my childhood I wonder how I survived at all,' McCourt's book began. 'It was, of course, a miserable childhood: the happy childhood is hardly worth your while. Worse than the ordinary miserable childhood is the miserable Irish childhood, and worse yet is the miserable Irish Catholic childhood.'

And with that bracing introduction to McCourt's early life in Brooklyn and in Limerick, *Angela's Ashes* became a global bestseller, acclaimed not only for its literary value but for its candor, for the Ireland Frank McCourt portrayed was not the Ireland of quaint villages, green landscapes, and smiling locals. The Ireland Frank McCourt described was, in a word, hidden. But no longer, not after *Angela's Ashes*. McCourt won a Pulitzer Prize and the affection of millions.

A year later, in 1998, Alice McDermott told the story of charming Billy Lynch of the Bronx, dead of the drink. There were secrets in his life, deceptions, an old love in Ireland whose very existence was kept hidden from him for years, for his friend thought it better that Billy think that God had taken her away because the truth – that she had taken his money and married somebody else – was too painful. But eventually what was hidden becomes known, and the story of the unremarkable life of Billy Lynch becomes a beautifully rendered portrait of romance, regret, and delusion. *Charming Billy* won the 1998 National Book Award for fiction.

That same year, the combined forces of the Disney Company and PBS produced a four-part documentary series called *The Irish in America: Long Journey Home*. Directed by Thomas Lennon, a future Oscar-winner, the six-hour film introduced new audiences to the searing experience of the Famine, the quiet dignity of immigrant laborers and domestics, and to the triumphs of politicians and union organizers. Paddy Maloney and Elvis Costello won a Grammy for the documentary's soundtrack.

Lennon's film, watched by millions, devoted nearly a quarter of its airtime to the Famine and its consequences for Ireland and for America. It premiered as scholars, writers, students and activists on both sides of the Atlantic were engaged in new efforts to extract meaning from the hunger and disruption and to reflect on hunger, want and misery hiding in plain sight in the developing world. Glucksman Ireland House was in the forefront of that effort, hosting a conference in 1995 on hunger to commemorate the 150th anniversary of An Gorta Mór and the ways it shaped and continued to shape Ireland and Irish America. At around the same time, then-Assemblyman Joseph Crowley successfully sponsored legislation in Albany requiring schools to teach the Famine, and historian Maureen Murphy developed a curriculum for use in New York's public and private schools. It was time, Crowley said, to give 'proper attention' to a human catastrophe that history had ignored.

Bob Scally presented his book, a study of the townland of Ballykilcline in Roscommon during the years of hunger, to Mary Robinson during Glucksman Ireland House's hunger conference in 1995. The book's title was *The End of Hidden Ireland*.

The new-found American interest in Irish themes created a ready-made audience for Irish and Irish-American films, plays, novels, and music throughout the 1990s and into the new century, from the already famous rockers of U2 to new voices, many of them based in New York – film directors Jim Sheridan and Terry George, writers Colum McCann, Colm Tóibín, Emma Donoghue, Emer Martin, and the young musicians who found a home at Glucksman Ireland House on Friday nights as part of the House's Blarney Star concert series. The work of playwrights Martin McDonagh, Marie Jones, Conor McPherson, Marina Carr, John Patrick Shanley and Sebastian Barry won enthusiastic reviews when they opened on the stages of New York.

Even as the Irish in America found new career and creative paths open to them in the late twentieth century, even as groups like the Irish Lesbian and Gay Organization were asking impertinent questions about identity and equality, two bastions of the New York Irish appeared to be unchanged and unchallenged, as profoundly and self-consciously Irish as they were a century earlier: The Fire Department of New York, and the Roman Catholic Church. One was about to experience unimaginable tragedy. The other, humiliating scandal.

On the morning of September 11, 2001, 343 New York firefighters were among the nearly 3,000 who perished in terrorist attacks against the United States. The assault on the World Trade Center and Pentagon, and the attack that was foiled over the skies of western Pennsylvania, were directed against America but the grief was global: Sixty-seven dead from the United Kingdom, twenty-eight from South Korea, forty-one from India, eighteen from Colombia, ten from Australia, along with

Clockwise from top left:
Music has been a vital part of the Glucksman Ireland House program. Pictured are Professor Mick Moloney and members of the Washington Square Harp and Shamrock Orchestra. ©NYU.

Director Jim Sheridan (right), whose films helped stir interest in all things Irish in the 1990s, with Ciaran O'Reilly, producing director of Irish Rep, a key part of the Irish revival in New York. Photo courtesy of James Higgins.

Legendary writer Mary Higgins Clark has been a guest at Glucksman Ireland House. Here she is with Patricia Harty, journalist and a member of the House's board. ©NYU.

Film director Terry George, Bono, and a fan. ©NYU.

about 2,500 Americans. No Irish nationals were among the dead, but the roster of the FDNY's fallen told a profoundly Irish story: the first deputy commissioner, William Feehan; the chaplain, Mychal Judge; a legendary deputy chief, Ray Downey; battalion chiefs named Ryan and McGovern and O'Hagan and Devlin; captains named Egan and O'Keefe and Farrelly, lieutenants named Phelan and Ahearn, and dozens with Irish names among the rank and file who joined their colleagues with roots in Italy and Scandinavia, the Caribbean and the Pacific, in the climb up those stairs to hell and who perished together when the towers came down.

There were police in those buildings, too: twenty-three officers from the New York Police Department and thirty-seven from the Port Authority police were among the dead. And inevitably there were Irish names among the fallen cops, for the Irish presence in law enforcement in New York remained vibrant even if not as dominant as it once was. Moira Ann Smith was the first police officer to respond to the stricken World Trade Center, and quickly assisted an office worker bleeding from the head. Somebody took her picture as she escorted the worker away from danger, and then she went back where she was needed. She was never seen again. On the day of her memorial Mass in St. Patrick's Cathedral the following February, on what would have been her 39th birthday, her husband James, also a police officer, and their 2-year-old daughter helped christen a Hudson River ferryboat as the *Moira Smith*, in her honor and as a symbol of the NYPD's sacrifice that day. The image of a gold Claddagh symbol appears on the ship's hull, next to her name. Another cross-Hudson ferryboat was christened the *Father Mychal Judge*, a remembrance of a remarkable Irish-American friar and all of his FDNY colleagues who gave their lives on that terrible morning.

The tragedy and sorrow of 9/11 blurred the divisions and identities that make New York such a turbulent, maddening and creative city. But as bagpipers assembled outside houses of worship throughout the city and its immediate suburbs in the weeks after the attacks, as the city paid

The Rev. Mychal Judge, a Franciscan and the son of immigrants from County Leitrim, was killed by debris when the South Tower of the World Trade Center collapsed on September 11, 2001. Firefighters gently carried his body from the North Tower lobby to nearby St. Peter's Church. REUTERS/Shannon Stapleton PM.

tribute to those who fell in service to others, there was an unmistakably Irish presence in the sorrow and the defiance.

The other persistently and proudly Irish institution in America, the Catholic Church, became enveloped in a scandal of historic proportions after the *Boston Globe's* Spotlight team discovered in early 2002 that dozens of predatory priests had been shuttled from parish to parish with the knowledge and approval of the archdiocese's mostly Irish hierarchy. The Church had championed, educated, comforted, and instructed generations of the Irish in America, but by the early years of the twenty-first century, its claims to moral leadership were shattered. The same process, for some of the same reasons, was unfolding in Ireland – the popularity of the sitcom *Father Ted* in the late 1990s would have been unthinkable even in the 1980s, a sign that Ireland was quickly moving away from the piety of previous generations. And a succession of government inquiries into clerical sexual abuse led to the previously unthinkable scene of a Taoiseach, Enda Kenny, condemning the Catholic hierarchy on the floor of the Dáil. The Church, he said in 2011, 'needs to be a penitent Church. A church truly and deeply penitent for the horrors it perpetrated, hid and denied.' Four years later, voters in the Irish Republic approved the legalization of gay marriage, the first country to do so by popular referendum.

Changed, utterly.

'There are still some of us left.' Pat Moynihan wrote those words, quoting a no-doubt apocryphal greeting from one Irishman to another in New York, in the early 1960s. For Moynihan, the greeting reflected Irish-American displacement in the middle of the twentieth century, delivered not with an ironic smile but with the grim and certain knowledge that a way of life was passing. And so it has. And so it hasn't.

Today an Irishman still is in residence on Madison Avenue behind the great cathedral named in honor of Ireland's patron saint. Irish societies rooted in the experience of nineteenth-century emigration still hold their dances and march behind their county banners, their annual awards dinners recorded for posterity on the pages of the *Irish Echo* or online on IrishCentral. The last three police commissioners in New York have been Irish-American. Across the river, the three most important politicians in Trenton are named Murphy, Sweeney and Coughlin.

There are still some of us left.

But then there are others who have crossed new thresholds in careers and culture, their journeys no longer tethered to the parish, the union hall, the expectations of the past. They have marched in a St. Patrick's Day Parade in Queens that proclaims itself open to all, they have explored

The lifeblood of the House: intellectually curious students who give the program its energy. ©NYU.

and interrogated the hyphen in their identity as never before, they have grasped opportunities denied their parents and grandparents, and they have decided that the book of Irish America is very much open and there are many more stories to write. The doctors and chief executive officers whose parents were cops and schoolteachers are writing those stories even now, to be read alongside the stories of late-night television hosts, political commentators, actors, novelists, journalists and historians unabashed about their Irish roots and yet unmistakably American. They are the legatees of the Irish-American revival of the late twentieth century, and their connection to Ireland is arguably stronger today than it was a quarter-century ago.

Glucksman Ireland House has presided over, benefited from, and inspired a quarter-century of questioning, commemorating, and preserving Irish-American identity and culture. The essays that follow offer reflections, some deeply personal, on all that Glucksman Ireland House has witnessed, and led, since that April day in 1993, when Lew and Loretta Brennan Glucksman opened a door on Fifth Avenue and invited in the world.

# Child of My Heart

## Playing for the Spirit
## of His Ancestors

# ALICE McDERMOTT

For my mother and her sisters, Brooklyn-born daughters of Irish immigrants, it was ComeAllYa music. Whenever my long-suffering grandmother found a touch of a traditional Irish tune on the radio, or placed one of her 78s on the 'victrola,' her children, New York sophisticates, would moan. Oh please, not that, not that ComeAllYa stuff – a term coined for the ubiquitous opening phrases of these mournful ditties: Come all you people, gather round, hear my tale, etc., etc.

My brothers and I, second generation Irish Americans growing up in the post-war suburbs of Long Island, came to share their distaste. Bing Crosby's Too-Ra- Loo-Ra-Loo-Ral or Galway Bay were unavoidable, especially at certain times of the year. And McGinty's Goat was a good song for a long car ride. As kids, we listened with some attention (and not a few reluctant tears) whenever my father – also first-generation Irish – sang the sad songs he'd learned from a musical Irish aunt. (The shot and shell were flying/he fought in his bravest style/and he died like an emerald Irishman/for the emerald isle.) But those pale, broad-faced tenors on Ed Sullivan or Lawrence Welk singing about the little piece of heaven that fell into the ocean ('Sure they called it Eye-RRR-Land'), or the Clancy Brothers belting out *The Wild Colonial Boy* in their awkward fisherman sweaters sent us into paroxisms of disdain.

Traditional music, the deedle-dum stuff of Aer Lingus ads and Lucky Charms commercials, sounded to our impatient American ears repetitive and clichéd. Stage Irish overkill. Cue *The Quiet Man.*

When my husband and I first visited Ireland with our own three children, our older son, at 12 already a budding musician, picked up a tin whistle as a souvenir.

At the music shop in Doolin, a helpful clerk handed him Darby's Farewell, the only CD recorded by Josie McDermott, the blind Roscommon whistle and flute player. (No relation – although to be Irish-American is to add: that I know of.)

'If you want to teach yourself to play,' the clerk said, 'all you need to do is listen to Josie.' But it was jazz, not trad, that was Will's musical obsession, and the CD languished for most of the year – dusted off annually for his little brother's wearing-of-the-green themed birthday parties on March 16, and, of course, for the other Patrick's feast day that followed.

And yet, somehow, traditional Irish music began to infiltrate the psyche of our youngest child. We're still not sure how to account for it. Looking back, we point to the haunting soundtrack of John Sayles' film *The Secret of Roan Inish*, a DVD Patrick loved even as a pre-schooler. We cite the music of The Pogues, Dropkick Murphys, Flogging Molly, U2, as it began to appear on his older siblings' playlists, bringing along with those adolescent-pleasing lyrics and the pounding ('turn that down') rhythms, hints of whistle and flute, *bodhrán* and uilleann pipes.

Whatever the reason, when he was about nine years old, Patrick found that souvenir tin whistle and began to teach himself to play – simply by listening to Josie. And then he asked us to find him a teacher. And then CDs by The Chieftans, Lúnasa, and Cherish the Ladies began to show up on his wish lists. As luck and coincidence would have it, a pub just a mile from our Bethesda home had a trad session every Monday night, and as a reward for homework completed, we'd bring him there to listen. Each week, before leaving the house, he would hand me his whistle and the small, handwritten list of tunes he had learned, with the instruction that I should keep both hidden in my purse until he worked up the courage to ask if he could sit in. After perhaps a year of such Mondays, he found that courage, and was welcomed into the circle of players, four-inch tune list and all, like a favorite son.

On the advice of his tin whistle teacher, we called flutist Hammy Hamilton on our next trip to Ireland. Hammy greeted Patrick in much the same way. The Irish music community, I was beginning to learn, was the very embodiment of a thousand welcomes. Although we were utter strangers, Hammy invited us to his Cork workshop, where he gave Patrick a leisurely seminar in flute making. We left with an excellent, if inelegant, practice flute made of aluminum pipe and industrial rubber. Hammy's advice: let Patrick learn to play on the practice flute before investing in a real one.

More lessons, then, more nights at the pub, more listening. One of the pub musicians, Mitch Fanning, had founded a group of young fiddle players called The Bog Band, and he invited Patrick to join them. Now there were rehearsals and performances and music festivals with his peers, a dedicated group of like-minded American kids, not all of them with Irish DNA, who, for reasons of their own, loved jigs and reels and marches and slow airs. ('You don't choose this music,' Mitch liked to say. 'It chooses you.') In the years to follow, there would be three Bog Band CDs, shows at the Smithsonian, The Kennedy Center, schools and hospitals, a field trip to play at Glucksman Ireland House, courtesy of the kindness of Don Meade, gigs at the Governor's mansion and the Vice-President's residence – when Martin O'Malley was the governor and Joe Biden the V.P.

In our house, we knew our young musician was awake every morning when we heard the trill of a whistle floating from his room.

As Patrick had gained more expertise, we'd put his name on what promised to be a two-year waitlist for a cocus-wood Irish flute handmade by Patrick Olwell of Virginia, flute maker for the likes of the Chieftans' Matt Molloy. One year into the wait, we received a call from Olwell in late November, a flute meant for another musician had just become available. A fine Christmas ensued.

On another family trip to Ireland, we went to Miltown Malbay for five days of classes and sessions during Willie Clancy Week. Patrick returned determined – perhaps it was the ghost of Willie Clancy himself to play the uilleann pipes as well. (If ever a good mother wants to put her maternal patience to the test, she should try the first few weeks of a child learning to play the uilleann pipes.) Lessons began via Skype with the kind and generous Bronx piper Jerry O'Sullivan – renowned in our family for telling our son, after they had played a rousing set together, 'There's hundreds to be made with this music, Patrick. Hundreds!' The piping of Seamus Ennis, captured in YouTube eternity, played constantly from the computer in Patrick's room.

At 13, he brought pipes, flute and whistle to his first mid-Atlantic fleadh, where the famous Galway flute player Mike Rafferty listened to him play three tunes on the uilleann pipes – the only competitor in his age group – and then slid the First Place medal to him with – yes, the full-fledged Irish cliché – a delighted twinkle in his eyes. Medals followed in the more populated fields of flute and whistle, and that summer, Patrick was off to Ireland for his first international competition at the Fleadh Cheoil.

There, on the night before he was to compete, we went to hear Finbar Furey at a local venue. Just a few months earlier, Finbar had visited Patrick's high school to play for a group of seniors in an Irish Studies class. The teacher had asked Patrick, still a freshman, to bring his flute and sit in as well. After the class, Finbar invited Patrick to his concert that evening, and at the encore, called him up to the stage. The two played a gorgeous set. When it was over, Finbar reached out to shake Patrick's hand and slipped him a $50 bill. 'You've earned it,' he said.

Photo courtesy of Alice McDermott.

Now, on the night before the competition in Tullamore, Finbar put his big hands on either side of Patrick's face. 'Listen to me,' he said. Finbar's face and voice were a perfect match. He had the beat-up good looks and the gruff brogue of a Hollywood Irish gangster, or bar fighter, or piper. 'When you play tomorrow, you're not playing for yourself,' Finbar said. 'You're not playing for your own ego. You're certainly not playing for the judges. You're playing for the spirit of your ancestors, who are making themselves known now, through you.'

Looking on, my husband and I, who had already vowed never to become hovering stage parents, nevertheless felt our hearts drop: wasn't this a heavy burden to place on the poor kid? The spirit of your ancestors? But our son felt no such weight. In fact, he told us that Finbar's injunction made him both determined to play his best and indifferent to whether or not he won. (Reader: he did, and he didn't).

It's the spirit of his ancestors became a family refrain – half joking, half sincere, flecked with a wry kind of wonder. 'Where do you think Patrick goes when he closes his eyes and plays the pipes?' a cousin asked after watching him on stage. He's communing with the spirit of his ancestors. At a session on another trip to Ireland, my brother marveled, 'How does he keep all these tunes in his head?' Spirit of his ancestors. 'He's more Irish than the Irish,' my mother took to telling her friends. 'We don't know where it comes from.'

Mitch Fanning, founder of The Bog Band, ran a week-long summer workshop, Musical Arts and Dance Week (MAD), and my husband and I took to offering our home as a B&B for attending faculty. Over the course of many summers, we found gathered at our kitchen table some of the world's best Irish musicians: Billy McComisky, Tony DiMarco, Lunasa's Cillian Vallely and Kevin Crawford (who, we were amused to discover, also announced he was awake with a whistle tune), Kevin Burke, Robbie O'Connell, Brian Conway, Rose Flanagan, Jerry O'Sullivan, Martin Hayes. Two generations removed from my Irish roots, I hosted these all-night sessions like some cottage colleen. I brewed pots of tea long into the wee hours, served slices of pie and cake, some wine and some whiskey, tapping my feet as the musicians, who had spent the day teaching, now played for themselves alone, for the joy of it.

Slowly, I found I was beginning to understand what Patrick had known intuitively: that this music, heard properly, defies its own clichés. That what seems repetitive to the uninitiated is, in fact, incisive, incantatory, not a recycling but a revisiting, a burrowing, a drilling down into the heart of a piece, an evocation of sorts. (I recalled the repetitious recitation of the rosary in the churches of my childhood.) I saw that some unspoken understanding, astonishing in its ease, its community, is brought to bear as each new tune is introduced and the musicians – sometimes after just a second's hesitation, heads bowed to listen – lift their instruments and seamlessly join in. It is a music bound to memory, not just figuratively, spirit of your ancestors, but literally – you won't find any pages of written music, 'little dots,' at an Irish session. As such, it is music that belongs simultaneously to the individual, to the musician's mental repertoire, and to the larger community with which it must be shared.

Along with those long nights of music there was also, inevitably, storytelling, and I began to hear in the refrains, the circling back, the convoluted asides and the unexpected retrievals of ordinary Irish conversation – which is to say of Irish storytelling – the same rhythms and surprises and rewards of the music. I saw something I had not seen before in my own memories of conversations around my grandmother's table, where, despite the first generation's disdain for that ComeAllYa stuff, there was, in the talk, Irish music nevertheless.

The spirit of your ancestors. In a community so small and so welcoming, connections are inevitable, of course, and it would surely be stage Irish overkill to make too much of them. On a graduation trip to Ireland with his high school class, Patrick stopped into a session at Matt Molloy's pub in Westport. And, of course, the man himself walked in. They played together on their Patrick Olwell flutes long into the night. In his first month at Fordham, Patrick was asked to play at a 9/11 memorial in St Paul's Church on Manhattan's west side, the same church where my father, who had died a decade before Patrick was born, had sung in the choir as a boy. One Christmas vacation Patrick received a call asking if he could play pipes as a musical birthday card at a retirement party in Georgetown. He agreed. 'And who should I say is sending the card?' he asked. 'Bono,' came the reply.

During a post-college internship on the island of Inis Meáin, an internship that had nothing to do with music, Patrick nevertheless found himself leading sessions in the pub and playing at Masses in the tiny church. With a dearth of experienced young musicians on the island – most of the youngsters head to the mainland for university and beyond – he found he was much in demand. Over trans-Atlantic Facetime conversations, he joked that he wasn't bringing Irish music to the island, he was only returning it.

In mid-June, my husband and I visited him on Inis Meáin. We were there for the feast of St John the Baptist, patron of the island. (I recalled an emigré priest once saying that the voice crying in the desert was surely an Irish tenor's.) As he had been doing throughout his nine-month stay, Patrick played for the special feast day Mass, providing back-up of sorts for the elementary school students with their tentative whistles and fiddles. But then, in the silence after Communion, he alone stood up in the pew. He lifted his flute and began to play Easter Snow, a slow air, one of my favorites. It was late afternoon, a cool day on the island. The small, whitewashed church was lit by candlelight and, through the narrow windows, the light of the overcast sky. In the pews around us there were old women in shawls and head scarves, figures from an ancient past, but there were also the younger residents of the island, indistinguishable in manner and dress from American suburbanites: farmers and fishermen, workers in the knitting factory, in the shop and the B&Bs. There were a few vacationers like ourselves. The lovely tune, aching, echoing, full of yearning, and sorrow, of the particularly Irish mix of grief and beauty, well suited the tiny church, the hour, that island sense, inevitable on a place as small as Inis Meáin, of the sea repeating its own endless refrain behind every human sound.

When the air came to an end, Patrick sat down again, the silence in the church richer now because of the tune he had played. In the renewed quiet, before the priest stood to pray, it was the memory of the music that lingered. The spirit of it. Something recalled. Something returned.

As we left the church, my husband and I agreed we had never heard him play so well.

In *The Celtic Twilight* Yeats describes listening to a fiddle player on a train, 'and though I am quite unmusical,' he wrote, 'the sounds filled me with the strangest emotions.'

> I seemed to hear a voice of lamentation out of the Golden Age. It told me we are imperfect, incomplete … It said that the world was once all perfect and kindly, and that still the kindly and the perfect world existed, but like a mass of roses under many spadefuls of earth. The faeries and the more innocent of the spirits dwelt within it and lamented over our fallen world in the lamentations of the wind-tossed reeds, in the songs of the birds, in the moan of the waves, and in the sweet cry of the fiddle …

It would have been easy enough for me, for my family, to lose a musical tradition that had hardly seemed our own. It's easy enough to shed any art, any bit of antique culture not fully to our taste, especially when that taste is so blithely uniformed. Easy enough to ignore the mass of roses under many spadefuls of earth. But, through some confluence of happenstance and luck, DNA, and all the mysterious elements that form a child, the music of our ancestors found its way into our household – music of lament, for sure, of the wind-tossed reeds, of the song of the birds and the moan of the waves, yes of course, but also the music of a kindly community, a witty, welcoming place where an art is practiced and passed on for the love of the art alone. A place, you might say, that's like a little piece of heaven – everybody now – and sure they called it Eye-RRR-Land . . .

Alice McDermott won a National Book Award in 1999 for her novel *Charming Billy*.

# Marching Towards the Future

# COLM TÓIBÍN

In the late 1980s a change began to come in Irish America. It began because of the new wave of Irish immigrants; it began because of changes that were happening in Ireland itself – new attitudes, new openness, fresh thinking, more tolerance, a new sense of what equality meant and what being Irish meant and implied.

In the week of St. Patrick's Day 1989 I came to New York for the first time in my life to report on what was happening in Irish America and to report on the city itself, why it was changing for the Irish and why it remained such an attractive destination for Irish people.

Things had begun that year, as they do in many organizations, with a split. The recently arrived Irish had discovered to their consternation that the St. Patrick's Day dinner, organized by the Friendly Sons of St. Patrick, was a male-only, black-tie affair. They decided that year not to attend, but to organize their own event in the Puck Building in SoHo, with a jazz band just to emphasize that there were many ways to be Irish. In earlier years, the annual St. Patrick's Day parades in Ireland itself, especially in Cork and Dublin, had been jazzed up. They no longer consisted of very cold people marching through the city wishing the end

The 1989 St. Patrick's Day Parade in New York was a genuinely historic event: For the first time in the parade's history, a woman, Dorothy Hayden Cudahy, served as grand marshal. Here she accepts congratulations from parade chairman Francis Beirne and Manhattan Borough President David Dinkins. Later that year, Dinkins became the first (and thus far only) African-American mayor of New York. Photo courtesy of Archives of Irish America, Bobst Library, New York University.

were nigh. Instead, it became a festival, with fireworks the night before, and the parade itself was led not by a dignitary or a politician but by someone from show business, someone everybody wanted to see. People brought their children into the city center on St. Patrick's Day so the family could enjoy watching the different floats in the parade.

Thus I was surprised, to say the least, at the St. Patrick's Day Parade in New York in 1989. There was almost no color at all, except for some green, no razzmatazz, no excitement. I fell in with a couple of politicians I knew who hailed from Longford and marched under the Longford banner. This was, in its way, a kind of disgrace as it was clear to everyone I met that I should have been marching behind the Wexford banner, since I come from there. (Little did I know that in the near future I would need to be marching under the gay banner, since I come from there, too. Our exclusion from the parade would become the burning issue in the decades that followed.)

Mostly men, we walked up Fifth Avenue. I was proudly told that the Irish parade was the only one that was allowed use Fifth Avenue on a weekday. Nothing much happened. People on the sidewalk looked on in a desultory way. There was nothing to applaud. Except that it was the first time that a woman – the radio host Dorothy Hayden Cudahy – was leading the parade as grand marshal. (There have been four others in the subsequent years, most recently Loretta Brennan Glucksman in 2018.) For a woman to be grand marshal, the by-laws had to be changed to allow members of the Ladies Ancient Order of Hibernians to be considered for this honor.

This change was not quick enough for many of the new Irish, however. Down at the Puck Building that night there was no green beer and a not a sign of a leprechaun. Instead, there were many young lawyers, accountants, engineers and other professionals, both women and men. They loved what New York could offer them now – a sense of the fast lane and the bright lights, high-paying jobs, the freedom of being away from home.

When I spent part of that day in an Irish radio station and then marching up Fifth Avenue, I did have a sense of old ghosts lingering, a sense that we were honoring the memory of Irish people coming to America in search of a last chance. A sense, too, of the Catholic Church as a place where these immigrants from Ireland could feel at home. (In subsequent years, three cardinals served as grand marshal: John O'Connor in 1995, Edward Egan in 2002, and Timothy Dolan in 2015.) As I walked toward the dinner in the Puck Building I bumped into an Irish-American man and his son whom I had met earlier in the day. They were in their tuxedos going to their all-male dinner. I felt almost ashamed even to hint to them that for us, the Irish born in Ireland, they looked like something strange from the past, alien to the way Ireland was now.

In the Puck Building, as the night wore on, there were no ghosts, there was no past. There were bright eyes and there was good food and there was sweet, soaring jazz. This event was being held to heighten the tone of the future rather than honor or mark the past. This was the Ireland of the Celtic Tiger making an early appearance. No one in this ballroom had emigrated for life. The young people here did not know where they would go next. America could be just a stop on their way to freedom. They might try London next, or transform Dublin in their own likeness.

Over the next week, I walked the streets of New York, went to the famous galleries, the famous stores, the theater. I came to the conclusion that I had made a mistake by booking my return flight on a Saturday since the previous day would be Good Friday and I presumed that most things would be closed in New York that day, as they were in Ireland. (The pubs in Ireland closed all day Good Friday; even the few supermarkets that opened were forbidden from selling alcohol.) I would be spending my last day, I believed, in a city where there was nothing to do.

I was surprised, to say the least, to find that the Metropolitan Opera was open on Good Friday with a production of Wagner's *Die Walküre*, which would begin at six o'clock in the evening and last for six hours. The cast would include two of my favorite singers – the soprano Jessye Norman and the mezzo Christa Ludwig. But when I went to the box office, I discovered that, since this was the season's first performance of *Die Walküre*, most of the seats were booked and the ones remaining were really expensive.

For five dollars, however, I could buy a standing room only ticket. Not only had I not seen these singers live – I knew their voices just from recordings – I had only once seen a Wagner opera performed, and that was in a concert performance without the costumes and the drama. I could not miss this chance.

On that Good Friday, I discovered that bars and restaurants and stores were fully open. The city was running as normal. Amazed by this, and feeling oddly liberated, I did some shopping and then got ready for my six-hour ordeal at the Met.

Despite my own lack of interest in religion that day, someone must have been praying for me. As soon as the lights went down in the Met, I saw that a single aisle seat was vacant. It was one of the best in the house. I watched for a while, and then pounced, moving towards it as though I had not only paid for it but sponsored it. This was the old, famous Met production of Wagner's Ring Cycle. The sets were old-fashioned and sumptuous, the lighting exquisite, the orchestra was utterly superb and the singing out of this world, the singers fully committed not only to the notes they sang, but to the darkening drama. Almost thirty years later, when I hear the opening ominous sound of that opera, I am back in my magical seat at the Met, an Irish American on his first Good Friday in New York, savoring all that gravity and grandeur, and no one to tell me that I had moved several notches above my station.

The problem, of course, was what to do when it was over. Could I just go home at midnight? This was, after all, my last night in New York. Earlier in the week, I had met an Irish friend who lived in the city and who said he was meeting other friends on the evening of Good Friday, but he just didn't know where. When I explained that I was going to the Met and would not be free until midnight, he said that was no problem. He had found a new trick, he said. From a pay phone he could call his own number, and using a code, change the message on his own answering machine voice mail system. Thus he would be able to let me know where he and his friends were.

This sounded like a sort of magic, the sort of thing that you could tell people at home that would make them feel awe at the newness and freshness of America. This innovation in how you could let people know what bar you were going to was far more interesting and far-reaching that any split in Irish-America.

That night, after my sojourn with German music, I found a humble pay phone, or coin-box, to use an Irish term. I put in my quarter and dialed the number. And there it was: the voice telling me that my friends and many others were to be found down in McManus's on Eighth Avenue between 19th Street and 20th Street.

Still exhilarated by the music, I got a taxi down through Manhattan, wondering why I had not left Ireland for here years before, wondering why in the name of God I was going home the next day. I got to the bar and found about twenty Irish people there, five or six of whom I knew.

As the night wore on, we toasted home, we toasted the Friendly Sons of St Patrick in all their future guises, but more than anything we toasted New York and the fact that the bar would be open until four in the morning on Good Friday. Some of the company went home before the bar finally served its last drinks; some stayed. Just coming up to four o'clock, some men who had been working for the city's Sanitation Department stopped by. Some of them were Irish; some were not. We had a last drink with them.

And then we stood out on the street as taxis raced by and the sound of the subways moving uptown and downtown could be heard below our feet. Irish-America was changing, we agreed, but it was not just that. That would work itself out. What was even more important perhaps was that the lure of New York for us would remain. One day you could march under the banner of Longford; that evening you could attend a dissenting dinner. One day you could spend six hours listening to

Wagner; later, you could spend four hours in an Irish bar. And, as I hailed a taxi to take me home, I wondered that anyone stayed in Ireland at all.

In the morning, when I was sober, I had other thoughts again. All the certainties of the previous night, the glee at spending a Good Friday so happily and carelessly, crumbled a bit as I tried to get ready to make my way to the airport. It was hard to be certain about anything. That first trip in that year of change in Irish America had the virtue at least of making me feel unsure.

Colm Tóibín is a novelist, playwright, critic and essayist whose works include *Brooklyn* and *The Master*.

# History, House
# and Home

# MARION R. CASEY

There is an old photograph of me with the Washington Square Arch in the background on the day I registered for an MA in History at New York University. What strikes me now is how prescient that photograph is: I am standing on the southeast corner of Fifth Avenue and Washington Square North.

If destiny has a GPS, then I was peering into the future from a point that has nurtured my career for more than thirty years. That twenty-something graduate student, fresh out of University College Dublin, did not anticipate going on to earn a doctorate in history from NYU, and certainly could not have predicted the creation of Glucksman Ireland House nine years later. And yet, if I were ever in the right place at the right time, it was that moment near the Arch on that day long ago.

In the 1980s, NYU's History Department was in 19 University Place. I don't recall how many times I walked through Washington Mews and passed the little townhouse on the Fifth Avenue end, then a private residence. I didn't yet know much about this tiny slice of the Village, but in the course of researching a paper on the old Sailors Snug Harbor,

I learned that this block of Washington Square North once was part of an estate owned by Captain Robert Richard Randall. He was an eighteenth-century privateer, the son of an immigrant from Limerick, and the rental income from this part of Manhattan went to support their pioneering philanthropic work with retired seamen.

Of all the real estate possibilities around the square, how did it come to pass that 1 Washington Mews was remade as Glucksman Ireland House in 1993?

In 2009, when Washington Square Park was undergoing an extensive renovation, the former yellow fever burial ground yielded a single headstone: James Jackson, a native of County Kildare, a banished United Irishman who died in New York in 1798. Could anyone have mapped the location of Irish Studies at NYU any better?

History rhymes.

I remember a graduate course at NYU on the relationship between great cities and literary culture, taught by a major historian who was vexed when I wanted to write about Joyce and *Dubliners*. Ireland and the Irish did not rank in his hierarchy of intellectual history. Nor was Ireland considered part of the Atlantic World, nor were the Irish part of anything but a discrete, limited moment in the history of the United States. It was despite such an environment that Bob Scally and Joe Lee brought Irish Studies out of the shadows and made NYU a major force in the global Irish Studies world in a single generation. Arguably, without the locus of Glucksman Ireland House and its generous, visionary patrons, it would have been a far slower evolution.

During my time at NYU, Irish America increasingly became the focus of sustained teaching and research for me. Soon I was sharing one of the offices in Glucksman Ireland House with Denis Donoghue. We alternated days, took turns at the desk, sat in the same chair. As

I filled the room with archival collections to be accessioned by Bobst Library and his order slowly ceded to my paper chaos, he was ever the consummate, good-humored gentleman. How many times had I heard it said at UCD that we should aspire to be like this renowned literary critic?

People and place in time and space.

Would I be the historian I am today without Glucksman Ireland House? It certainly has given me the stability to mature as a scholar and the leeway to practice public history, to build the Archives of Irish America, to document the durability and elasticity of ethnic identity through oral history, to teach, research and publish across multiple countries, centuries, and perspectives. I have been unfettered by traditional academic disciplines and therefore able to contribute to the development of a dynamic field of study – call it Irish America or American-Irish or the Irish in America or the Irish and America very broadly defined – that did not exist twenty-five years ago.

Glucksman Ireland House has also been a bridge from which to move back and forth between the academy and the community. This has illuminated the understanding of my own roots as the child of immigrants and as a first-generation college student in one of the richest ethnic and racial metropoles in the world. Being Irish and teaching about the Irish has given me a clarity about the city I call home, about contemporary developments here and abroad, and about relationships among people of all colors and creeds. Far from being limiting, it has been liberating.

For a quarter-century, 1 Washington Mews has been my townland and *tigín*. Some of the most enduring friendships of my life have been forged over cups of tea within its walls. I was married there, and Bob Scally gave the toast. Joe Lee is my daughter's godfather.

Time, space, people, place. History, house, home.

'May the roof overhead be well thatched and those inside be well matched' *go brách*.

Marion R. Casey is a clinical associate professor of history at Glucksman Ireland House and was co-editor of *Making the Irish American: History and Heritage of the Irish in the United States*.

# The Importance of
# Being Frank

# DAN BARRY

By day he was the captivating teacher, recounting his tragicomic childhood to help students recognize the Homeric epics of their own young lives. And by night he was the tavern raconteur, spinning tales so beguiling that accomplished denizens would allow through their laughter and tears that it was good, Frank, very good. You really ought to write it down.

Now imagine if this silver-tongued storyteller had not written it down. Imagine instead that he had joined New York City's legions of literary lotus-eaters, whose half-written manuscripts and bar-napkin scribbles could dam the Hudson with unrealized promise.

No Angela, then; only ashes.

But Frank McCourt, when well into his 60s, somehow mustered the discipline to write it all down, and came up with art. His memoir, *Angela's Ashes*, published in 1996, charmed the world, spawned a memoir glut, and drove a blackthorn spike through the twee heart of the auld country Neverland for which Irish America so often pines.

This moment of literary destiny followed a protracted period of gestation. When Frank was a spit of 13, navigating impoverishment

Frank McCourt, seen here with Loretta Brennan Glucksman at an event in the House, burst onto the global literary scene in 1996 with his unforgettable memoir, *Angela's Ashes*. The book was awarded a Pulitzer Prize in 1997. ©NYU.

and just recovered from typhoid fever, he was assigned an essay by a brilliant and encouraging headmaster whose pronounced limp had earned him the sobriquet of 'Hoppy.' After reading the essay, according to McCourtian lore. At a monthly salon the teacher is said to have said: 'McCourt, you're a literary genius. When you get older, go to America. They will appreciate you there.'

You can hear the schoolyard taunts even now. *Oh you're a genius! Say something in genius …*

For many years, though, Frank McCourt produced nothing of genius; nothing to appreciate. At one point in early middle age, he tried to pin down memories of his Brooklyn–Limerick boyhood with typewriter strikes against onion-skin paper, making lists of people, of houses, of moments with epiphanic potential. Called 'If You Live in a Lane,' these jottings were little more than an outline of an outline of what was to come. He shoved it into the struggling writer's oubliette, the desk drawer.

A few years later, Frank and his younger brother Malachy, by then a successful actor, publican, and raconteur, were entertaining friends with riffs on the characters they knew and the songs they sang in that squalid Limerick lane of their childhood. Soon they were riffing on a dusky stage above an East Side saloon, having too much fun to address elemental matters of stagecraft, such as structure or length.

Practically ordered by the eminent actress and director Geraldine Fitzgerald to write the material down, Frank set to it, and a relatively successful sketch play, *A Couple of Blaguards*, was born. It included a scene that later figured in *Angela's Ashes*, one in which young Frank overeats during a post-Mass breakfast, vomits in the yard, and sends his grandmother into paroxysms of worry:

'Look what he did. Thrun up his First Communion breakfast! Thrun up the body and blood of Jesus! I have God in me backyard! Oh what am I going to do?'

Still, Frank was falling far short of Hoppy's predictions, if not his own expectations. This sense was being reinforced in the Lion's Head tavern, where the covers of books written by habitués festooned the walls, as well as in the classroom, where students would occasionally return his volley of a dare to write their life stories down.

'It sort of comes back at you if you are urging them to write their stories,' Ellen McCourt, his wife, said. 'And then they ask what have you written – and you have nothing to show for it.'

Frank traveled a bit, did some acting, and wrote a couple of modest pieces for the *Village Voice*, including an ode to the notable urinals of New York. When his brother Malachy had to cancel a commitment with the History Theatre in St. Paul, Minnesota, Frank agreed to fill this sudden hole in the theater's schedule with a one-man show that further refined some of his stories from childhood. First in the classroom and now on the stage, he was listening to audience reaction, honing the language, learning what most resonated.

Still.

Ellen, then an executive in public relations, had been encouraging Frank since forever to write. As Malachy later told Jim Dwyer of *The New York Times*: 'Ellen didn't tell him to go back to work, you have nothing to say. She said: Go for it.'

Ellen remembers the very moment when her husband finally resolved to write it down – to write his damned book! It was in June 1994, and they were renting a house in the Delaware Water Gap area of eastern Pennsylvania. One of their guests already had written a couple of books, and another had just signed a contract with a large publisher. Frank was 'enormously envious,' she recalled.

A few months later, Ellen and a friend were sitting on the deck of that same Pennsylvania getaway, sipping wine and admiring an autumnal view of the Delaware River below. Frank emerged from the house and began to read the first two pages of the manuscript he was working on.

The beginning was almost exactly as it would appear in *Angela's Ashes*. 'By the time he wrote it down, it was fixed in his mind,' Ellen said.

Frank, then, returned.

Sitting at a wooden table in the apartment he shared with Ellen on East 18th Street, or by the fireplace in the barn of the house they bought in the Poconos, he returned to the Brooklyn and Limerick of the 1930s and 1940s: the poverty, the begging, the sibling deaths, the father's abandonment, the mother's sacrifice. ('Bridie laughs. Oh, Angela, you could go to Hell for that, and Mam says, Aren't I there already, Bridie?')

People would say to Ellen: So, you married a retired high school teacher. What's he doing now?

Well, he's writing a book.

Oh. Well, uh, good for him.

But Frank kept writing, setting as his deadline the 30th of November – the birthday of Jonathan Swift. He wrote in longhand in spiral notebooks, using one side to jot down names, locations, and incidents, and the other to unfold his narrative. Then the former army clerk typist would type up his manuscript on an early-generation Apple computer.

What happened next is more McCourtian lore. At a monthly saloon gathering of the like-minded known as the First Friday, the novelist Mary Breasted Smyth asked Frank what he was working on, and his answer – my miserable childhood – suggested a grave misreading of the book-buying public. But she asked to read what he had written, instantly recognized the fresh genius of it, and connected him with a literary agent. Soon his words, long in coming, had secured for Frank a $125,000 advance from Scribner.

So much would happen in the years to come. The international success; the Pulitzer Prize; the movie; the backlash alleging hyperbole, tempered by the overwhelming recognition that the literature of truth had been achieved. Serious illness met with grace and humor, followed by death, in 2009, at the age of 78.

But first there was the evening of November 30, 1995, in a certain second-floor apartment on East 18th Street. Ellen arrived home from work to find Frank waiting for her. A bottle of champagne was uncorked. And then, with his wife by his side, the retired schoolteacher typed out the last word to his memoir for the ages: 'Tis.

Dan Barry is a Pulitzer Prize-winning reporter for *The New York Times* and the author of several books, most recently, *This Land: America, Lost and Found.*

# How the Irish Challenged American Identity

## An Immigrant Group's History Lessons for Today

# HASIA R. DINER

As someone who has devoted her scholarly career to studying immigration and ethnicity as forces which shaped American history, I think it is obvious why Irish history matters. There should be no need to justify it. But on the other hand, merely going through the process of justification makes the patently obvious even more so. The narrative of the Irish experience in America lays bare some of the most essential elements of the larger history. Looking at that history, from the eighteenth century to the present, exposes some key issues with which the nation still struggles.

Now, it could be possible to say what I just said about any of the many immigrant populations that planted themselves in this new society and went through the many ordeals attendant upon settlement including the struggle for economic security, institution formation, experimenting with forms of self-defense against hostility, maintaining relationships with 'back home,' and participating in the profound cultural transformations which came with the passage of time. All went through it but the Irish did it first and they provide us with the best of examples. If one had to choose a single population from which to

Tammany Hall politicians like Al Smith, shown here with Franklin Roosevelt, built bridges to immigrant groups beyond Irish Catholics, and helped show what it meant to be an American in the early twentieth century. Photo courtesy of the Franklin D. Roosevelt Library and Museum.

tell the story of all immigrant groups, the women and men who left Ireland and came to America provide us with the most dramatic and most exemplary case.

The Irish experience in labor offers the clearest glimpse into the universal immigrant story. Put simply, Irish hands and bodies did the work Americans would not do but work which Americans deemed essential. In the eighteenth century this involved newcomers from Ulster settling and carving out towns and farmlands at the edge of the frontier, a bloody war zone. Other Americans, those of English origins, eschewed those mountainous lands as too poor, too difficult to farm, and too close to the fight against the native peoples. Ulster's people took up this territory to essentially protect urban dwellers and those closer to the coast from what they defined as an existential threat to their lives and property.

From the 1820s on, immigrants from the other parts of Ireland, primarily Catholics from the south, provided the muscle which fueled America's transportation and industrial revolutions, as well as its urban development. Taking the most dangerous and arduous jobs, they built the canals, laid the railroad tracks, blasted the mountains, tended the machinery in the factories, mined the coal, among other nearly herculean chores which facilitated the dynamic growth of the American economy. Irish women, ubiquitously referred to as 'Bridget,' washed, laundered, cooked, cleaned, and tended the children of white middle-class Protestant American families, liberating the women of those families from household toil. In their liberation, the employers of Irish servant women in turn changed American religion, culture, and politics. But they could secure the vote, raise money for charity, crusade against slavery, educate themselves, and redefine religious life only because Irish women did the work at home.

By the latter part of the nineteenth century, Irish-American men put out the all-too-frequent fires that ravaged American cities, provided the law and order which made urban life bearable, while Irish women in New York, Chicago, Boston and elsewhere taught the millions of children of the next waves of immigrants. Other Irish women tended to the sick as nurses, in both Catholic and municipal hospitals, offering the nation a first modicum of public health.

Irish women and men became advocates for the rights of workers, sounding the call for a living wage, invoking the dignity of labor. They brought us Labor Day and labor laws and they pressed for state intervention on the part of workers in the face of the power of capital. Simultaneously, the Irish political machine, Tammany Hall in New York and its equivalents around the country, served as powerful engines to foster immigrant male integration. Each new population which crested onto American shores – Italian, Polish, east European Jews and so many more – became American through the efforts of the Irish ward bosses and block captains who traded votes for patronage and favors. American progressives abhorred the Irish political machine, thinking it corrupt, but those organizations did much to bring new immigrants into the mainstream.

So, too, I think it is fair to say that Irish immigrants, the Catholic majority, forced America to live up to its constitutional principle embedded in the First Amendment, which guaranteed religious freedom and state neutrality when it came to matters of the spirit. But for the vigorous, often militant, behavior of Irish Catholics, both prelates and the laity, who challenged the encrusted Protestant hegemony which unofficially – and at times officially – declared America a Christian and a Protestant nation, the United States would never have become as religiously diverse and free as it did. As the first sizable group of non-Protestants to arrive in the United States, the Catholic Irish challenged the American self-image as a Protestant nation. Beyond just numbers, the Irish immigrants' devotion to their faith and the Catholic Church's power and brilliance in organizing neighborhood life pushed the nation to make the wall between religion and civic life increasingly thicker and less porous.

Even before independence and the first wave of Catholic immigration from Ireland, the United States put in place social, cultural, and political policies which demonized Catholics and therefore deprecated and disadvantaged the Irish – newcomers as well as their American-born daughters and sons. But since these victims fought back and won, they created, probably not intentionally, an increasingly large space, indeed an equal one, for other religious outsiders. Those later arrivals came with faith traditions that seemed to Americans to be inconsistent with what being American meant. But these subsequent non-Protestants and non-Christians reaped the benefits of Irish militancy in the nineteenth century. Their willingness to challenge American Protestantism paved the way for the flourishing of Judaism. In our own day, their legacy should be seen as a bulwark against Islamophobia.

I hope, as an American historian – and, frankly, as an American citizen (and the child of immigrants) – deeply troubled about the political and cultural trends roiling us today, that this story can teach us something. The Irish could not have been more outsiders in America. They could not have been more reviled or consigned to less difficult labor. But they challenged the economic, political, and cultural status quo. They made America a different and better place. And we should do so, too, in our day.

Hasia R. Diner served as interim director of Glucksman Ireland House, 2017–18, and is the Paul and Sylvia Steinberg Professor American Jewish History at New York University.

# Looking Back,
# Moving Forward

# PETER QUINN

Richard Croker and Jacob Riis had little in common. Riis was born in Denmark and gained fame as a crusading journalist and social reformer. His shocking account of life in New York's slums, *How the Other Half Lives*, stirred the national conscience. Irish-born Croker grew up in a shantytown on the fringes of the city, joined a gang, became a political enforcer and rose to be the leader (a.k.a. boss) of Tammany Hall. He earned a reputation for his toughness, bluntness and legendary greed.

The differences between Croker and Riis included their views of New York's tenement districts and their inhabitants. Riis chronicled their impoverished and miserable living conditions in hope of mitigating them. In the case of the Irish, he was less than optimistic. 'The Celt,' he wrote, 'falls most readily victim to tenement influences ... his progress henceforth [will be] along the line of the tenement.'

Croker was more sanguine. In an interview with an English journalist, he asserted that the city's streets and alleyways need not be a dead end. The way out was through political organization. Tammany found its strength there, he said, because it recognized 'there are men in the gutter, and we have to go where they are if you are to do anything for them.'

Riis's concern for the poor was heartfelt, while Croker's cynical self-interest can never be discounted. Yet both men held part of the truth: Riis, the poor's plight; Croker, their potential power. Reformers pursued moral uplift and reform from above. Tammany worked the streets, turning foreigners into citizens, and shepherding them to the polls. As the city's ur-immigrants and bottom dwellers, whose progress was 'along the line of the tenement,' the Irish regarded the precincts of the poor and lower classes not as areas for study or reform, but as neighborhoods rich with voters whose loyalty had to be won.

Contra Boss Croker, The Society of St. Tammany or the Columbian Order in the City of New York – to give the famous machine its full name – didn't have to stoop to the gutter, at least not very far. It grew up there. Corrupt as it often was, Tammany made sure never to condescend. The Hall offered the other half (which was often more like two-thirds) what reformers and the government of the day didn't or wouldn't: jobs, relief and, above all, respect.

The journey of the Irish from downtrodden peasantry to America's first underclass to consummate urban politicians began in the catastrophe of the Great Hunger. Under the best of circumstances, the transfer of deprived and traumatized rural masses from a deeply traditional, rigidly hierarchical society into the free-wheeling economy of an urbanizing, fast-industrializing republic was problematic. The Irish arrived under the worst. Between 1845 and 1855, a million died and two million, a quarter of the country, left.

In his 1849 novel, *Redburn*, Herman Melville drew a vivid picture of 'the hard and bitter lot' of Famine Irish packed below deck on a ship bound from Liverpool to New York. He also posed the vexing predicament they faced on landing: 'How, then, with these emigrants, who 3,000 miles from home, suddenly found themselves deprived of brothers and husbands, with but a few pounds, or perhaps but a few shillings, to buy food in a strange land?'

The unraveling the Famine brought about was reflected in the disorganized, deprived state of the newly arrived, seen by many as a permanent underclass. For these immigrants, the institutional infrastructure and informal networks that came to define Irish America were largely nonexistent. Their foreignness was exacerbated not only by their numbers, poverty, traditions – and in some cases their Irish language – but by a religion long the bête noir of Anglo-Saxon Protestants and the target of intense evangelical campaigns on both sides of the Atlantic.

The eponymous protagonist of Harold Frederic's intriguing 1894 novel *The Damnation of Theron Ware* summed up a widely shared, long-held view of the Irish that lingered into the twentieth century: 'He took it for granted that in the large cities most of the poverty and all the drunkenness, crime, and political corruption were due to the perverse qualities of this foreign people – qualities accentuated and emphasized in every evil direction by the baleful influence of a false and idolatrous religion.'

The rabidly anti-immigrant American Party (better known as the Know Nothings) transformed a visceral nativist backlash into the largest third party in American history. Riots broke out in Philadelphia. New York elected a nativist mayor. By 1855, the American Party controlled the legislatures of every New England state. Addressing the Massachusetts legislature that year, Governor Henry Gardner decried immigrants as the main source of beggary and criminality, and compared the 'insidious foreign influx to our shores' to the barbarians who overthrew the Roman Empire.

The immigrants' one source of capital was abundance of numbers. But so long as they remained an amorphous, ill-formed agglomeration – a mob – the ability to gain power and employ it to advantage, or at least prevent it from being used to their disadvantage, was beyond reach. Their change in fortune was primarily owed to the forceful and formative leadership of John Hughes, the archbishop of New York and native of County Tyrone.

An image of Archbishop John Hughes, the Tryone native who helped reorganize the Irish in New York during and after the Famine. © Alec Henson/NYU.

The Catholic Church that became synonymous with Irish America was of Hughes's making. Contentious and fearless, he was as much Irish chieftain as Christian churchman. He fought with laity, Jesuits, nativists, politicians, and city fathers. He crushed dissent and scorned his enemies. What he lacked in tactfulness, he made up for with fierce devotion to the welfare and future of his immigrant flock.

Unlike the devout, obedient and disciplined parishioners of later years, the congregants Hughes took charge of practiced the pre-Famine religion of the Irish countryside, a mélange of Celtic folk beliefs and Catholic practice. Their contact with priests and the sacraments was sporadic. By what often seemed sheer force of will, Hughes brought about a revolution. He built churches and schools, opened orphanages and hospitals, expanded the seminary, founded a university, and began the construction of St. Patrick's Cathedral.

The parish became a center of Irish life, secular as well as religious, a community where immigrants felt welcome and safe, and confraternities and sodalities fostered a sense of belonging. Over the next century, Catholic New Yorkers identified themselves not by street or neighborhood, but by parish.

Hughes's impact wasn't only ecclesiastical. He was the first to form the Irish into a powerful voting bloc capable of making itself heard. He wielded it like a club, making alliances with different parties, threatening retaliation against those who crossed him. In the process, he taught his followers the indispensable importance of a disciplined, coherent political organization to defend and advance their interests.

Half a century after Hughes's death, Tammany sachem and sage George Washington Plunkitt posited that 'the Irish was [sic] born to rule.' The truth was otherwise. In Ireland, a crushed and exploited peasantry fell in behind Daniel O'Connell, who organized Europe's first mass political movement. Though his efforts came apart in the face of Famine and British repression, he bequeathed an invaluable lesson in the power of organization. Hughes drove it home.

Irish organizational skills were not a function of the gene pool. Rather, they grew out of oppression and dispossession. History taught that privilege didn't yield to scattered pleas and solitary protests. In a democracy, power accrued to those who could consistently summon to the polls a loyal, reliable body of voters, and that required one thing above all. In the words of Bronx County leader Ed Flynn, the son of an Irish immigrant, 'In any political organization, as in any army, numbers aren't enough. There must be discipline.'

For the Irish in America, parochial was never a pejorative. It applied equally to politics and religion. The focus of people long accustomed to living on the edge, with their searing memories of ruinous want, was on security. In the days before the welfare state, when the social safety net was a threadbare of private charities, the neighborhood clubhouse was the best – sometimes only – hope of assistance. The lesson wasn't lost on those who followed. Tammany stayed in power long after the Irish ceased to make up the bulk of the electorate.

Patronage was a reward of loyalty and an incentive. Church and clubhouse doubled as employment agencies and hiring halls (as did saloons). Public jobs were a first rung on the economic ladder. They offered security and benefits the unskilled and under-educated couldn't find elsewhere. During times of inevitable, periodic economic bust, they were a last refuge. When patronage lost its sway, the Irish continued to place special value on public-service employment. In many families, civil service was elevated to a form of civil religion.

From the time the Irish first arrived, they were viewed as a source of cheap labor. While nativist workmen accused them of undercutting wages and stealing jobs, employers welcomed them for their willingness to take what work was available, however dirty, dangerous or exhausting. One New York grandee labeled the Irish as 'the hod-carrying race.' The elite, whose lifestyle depended on a servant class, labeled their maids with the collective moniker 'Bridgets.'

The reputation of the Irish for brawn and hard work was matched by suspicion at their lack of deference and proclivity for agitation, opposition and organization. As early as the 1820s, troops were called on to deal with Irish canal diggers. In Pennsylvania in the 1870s, faced with the crushing of their union, coal miners revived the Molly Maguires, a secret society that fought for tenant farmers in Ireland. The Mollies waged class warfare with a campaign of terror and intimidation ruthlessly put down by mine owners.

The scars of the Famine and a tradition of resisting the landlord class prepared the Irish for a lead role in the battle between labor and capital. Under Terence Powderly, the child of Irish immigrants, the Knights of Labor pioneered unionism on a national scale. Mother Jones, a Famine immigrant from Cork, became a legendary embodiment of working-class militancy. Driven by the exploitation and deprivation she saw around her, the Bronx-bred daughter of Irish immigrants, Elizabeth Gurley Flynn, was a founder of the American Communist Party. George Meany, a fellow Bronx Irish American, headed the far more cautious and powerful AFL-CIO.

The parochialism that often characterized Irish America has come in for criticism, much of it justified. It easily slipped into racial and ethnic exclusivity, fostered conformity and stifled individual expression. And yet, given that the ordinary challenges of emigration were vastly increased by the conditions of those who left and the hostility they faced when they arrived, the options were few, if any. The reorganization they undertook wasn't the result of planning or premeditation. Parish, clubhouse and union hall were built of necessity. All had their roots in Ireland. All had flaws. They imposed restrictions as well-presented opportunities.

In the end, whatever their faults, they provided the Irish the security and resources to take their place in American society and make significant contributions to its progress. Adrift in the maze of the megalopolis, the uprooted immigrants whom Melville pitied reconstituted themselves in an urban village that served as bulwark and battering ram, a space in which to regroup, find their bearings and clear the way for others to follow.

Over time, as Irish Americans pushed ahead, the pressures and challenges of assimilation made remembering more a luxury than priority. The immigrants' descendants focused on an American future, not on reliving a calamitous, traumatic past. Once seen as immiscible outsiders, they breached the walls that barred their forebears from the nation's top ranks of the influential and powerful. The great-grandson of Famine immigrants was elected the first president from outside the closed circle of Anglo-Saxon Protestants. Though they never vanished, the hard truths of struggle and survival faded into romance and sentiment.

The official opening of NYU Glucksman Ireland House in 1993 marked a new departure in the evolution of Irish Studies and in the relationship between Ireland and Irish America. Instead of appendage or afterthought, Irish history and culture were elevated to a central focus. For the first time, Irish America was brought out of the shadows and made the subject of academic attention and serious scholarship. Time-worn stereotypes – favorable and unfavorable – were challenged. The groundbreaking conference on hunger that Glucksman Ireland House hosted in 1995, on the 150th anniversary of the Great Hunger, ended a long silence and initiated a conversation that continues to grow more vibrant and relevant.

In the quarter-century since it opened its doors, Glucksman Ireland House has helped prompt a new appreciation of Irish identity, in all its myriad manifestations, throughout the global diaspora. The bond between Ireland and Irish America has been renewed and reinforced. Artists and writers are engaged in an unprecedented transatlantic exchange that is bringing new life to traditional culture and fostering innovative and revolutionary forms of expression. Today, there is widening interest in the relevance of Irish Studies to the colonial and post-colonial experiences of emerging societies.

The dream proclaimed on O'Connell Street in 1916 asserted the right of Ireland to resume its place among the nations of the world. Glucksman Ireland House provides a home for that dream in the heart of New York City, at the global crossroads of people and ideas. It welcomes the 'exiled children in America' and from across the diaspora, as well as all interested in understanding what it means to be Irish. Whatever the political winds, it is committed to build bridges that enable, encourage and expand an open-ended, generous, multicultural conversation that knows no boundaries or walls.

Novelist and essayist Peter Quinn is a member of the Glucksman Ireland House board and is the author of *Banished Children of Eve* and the Fintan Dunne trilogy of historical detective novels.

# A Season of Anniversaries

## Taking the Lead in Commemorating Famine and Rising

# MAUREEN MURPHY

In the quarter-century since the founding of Glucksman Ireland House, the Irish around the world have paused to recall and re-examine two of the most fateful events in modern Irish history: The Great Famine and the Easter Rising. The House played a key role in setting the stage for scholarly activity and public events in New York tied to the Famine's 150th anniversary and the centennial of the Rising.

Glucksman Ireland House was well positioned to take a leadership role for the Famine commemorations, even though the program was in its infancy in the mid-1990s. That's because the House's first director, Robert Scally, a son of Irish immigrants and a scholar of migration, was finishing his book *The End of Hidden Ireland. Rebellion, Famine & Emigration, 1832–1848* (1995), a study of the townland of Ballykilcline.

Scally's great contribution to Famine commemoration – not just in New York, but throughout the Irish disaspora – was his decision to connect hunger and deprivation in mid-nineteenth-century Ireland to the very same issues in the late twentieth century. Under his leadership, Glucksman Ireland House sponsored an international conference on world hunger in May 1995. Mary Robinson, the President of Ireland, came to New York to deliver one of the conference's keynote addresses, in which she noted that in 1993, more than 12 million children under the age of 5 died of famine in the developing world. In another keynote address, economist Amartya Sen examined the connections between drought and famine, making a connection between world hunger and climate conditions. (Sen went on to win the Nobel Prize for Economics in 1998.)

The hunger conference provided the appropriate context for an effort to bring the Famine and its lessons into the classrooms of New York. When my colleague at Hofstra University, Alan Singer, and I submitted an application to the New York State Education Department to write The Great Irish Famine Curriculum, we described our proposal as an opportunity to use the Famine as a model to teach about hunger and homelessness. We asked Bob Scally to serve as a member of our Advisory Board, and Bob facilitated a teleconference at Glucksman Ireland House with our Irish partners to discuss our plans for the curriculum.

The result was a comprehensive document of some eighteen hundred pages sent to all schools, public and private, throughout New York State. The curriculum includes a lesson plan on hunger in Somalia and the story of Frederick Douglass's visit to Ireland during the early stages of the Famine, along with an array of student activities that seek to tie together the suffering in Ireland a century-and-a-half ago with issues of poverty, injustice and starvation in the modern world.

Not long after the conference, when I was invited to join the design team for a Famine memorial in Battery Park City, I again sought to not simply memorialize hunger in Ireland but to bring attention to starvation around the world. Forty percent of the memorial's text is made up of quotes describing hunger in other times and other places – there are quotations in audio loops in Amharic, German, Irish, Russian and Spanish.

The Glucksman Ireland House conference also had an impact on another Famine memorial, this one in Westchester County. The founder

Glucksman Ireland House commemorated the centennial of the Easter Rising with a two-day conference in downtown Manhattan that attracted scholars and guests from both sides of the Atlantic. ©NYU.

and president of the Great Hunger Foundation in Westchester, the late Eleanor McDonald, drew her inspiration from the lessons she learned at the conference.

A little less than two decades after the hunger conference, Glucksman Ireland House again took the lead in preparing the way for a consequential anniversary, the centennial of the Easter Rising of 1916. Under the direction of Joe Lee, who had succeeded Scally as the head of Glucksman Ireland House in 2002, the House created an ad-hoc committee to plan a series of public programs, including a conference that would attract scholars from around the world. The House's 2014 Ernie O'Malley Lecture was transformed into a two-day symposium that attracted more than two dozen prominent scholars who discussed modern Ireland and revolution, setting the stage for the events and commemorations to come.

The 1916 centenary offered New York's Irish-American community an opportunity to come together to plan and schedule events in such a way as to support each other's efforts. Glucksman Ireland House played the leading institutional role in coordinating and collaborating with other Irish organizations in the city where so much planning and fundraising for the Rising took place – New York.

Invoking the Easter Proclamation's acknowledgment of support from Ireland's 'exiled children in America,' the Irish in New York developed exhibitions, lectures, lesson plans, and conferences focused on the Rising and especially on the role of Irish New Yorkers in the planning and financing of the rebellion. A booklet of commemorations throughout the city listed fifty-six events, beginning with an evening of traditional music at Glucksman Ireland House on September 17, 2015 and concluding with a return to NYU, to the Cantor Film Center, for a screening of a documentary, *1916: The Irish Rebellion*, produced by the University of Notre Dame and featuring Glucksman Ireland House director, Joe Lee.

The House sponsored ten events and co-sponsored two with the American Irish Historical Society and the Battery Heritage Foundation. The annual Ernie O'Malley Lecture featured Francis M. Carroll's 'The United Irish League of America 1910–1918: The Center Did Not Hold.' And on April 21 and 22, Glucksman Ireland House sponsored a two-day conference entitled, 'Independent Spirit: America and the 1916 Easter Rising,' featuring leading scholars as well as several graduate students in NYU's master's program in Irish and Irish-American Studies. The conference led to the publication of *Ireland's Allies: America and the 1916 Easter Rising* edited by Miriam Nyhan Grey. In documenting the role of the New York Irish in the Rising and its aftermath, *Ireland's Allies* is a major contribution to our understanding of what happened in Ireland in 1916.

The New York centennial commemorations were complementary to those in Ireland but also were uniquely Irish-American. Dublin opted to celebrate the anniversary on Easter Monday, which fell on March 28, 2016. New York marked the occasion on the actual date of the Rising, April 24, with a ceremony in Battery Park City followed by a day of lectures, readings, and performances.

The centennial events in New York (and in Ireland itself) offered a sharp contrast with the ways in which the fiftieth anniversary of the Rising was celebrated in 1966. Those commemorations reflected the overarching presence of Eamon de Valera, a veteran of 1916, in Irish civic life. The 1966 anniversary focused almost exclusively on the Rising's leaders, all of whom were executed in the weeks after rebel forces surrendered in Dublin. The ceremonies fifty years later, in a very different Ireland – and a very different Irish America – were more inclusive. They included discussions of the role that women played, the toll civilians paid during the fighting in Dublin, and the plight of Irish soldiers who fought and died in France as members of the British Army. These issues complicated the storyline that was celebrated in 1966 and recognized groups that had been written out of the Rising's narrative.

There were also special aspects of the anniversary for the Irish-American community. It was the last chance to identify, document and chronicle the role of members of the 1916 generation who worked in America to support the nationalist movement before, during and after the Rising. This was a chance to honor those unreported or underreported persons and events.

Again, Glucksman Ireland House provided the leadership, and demonstrated, not for the first time, the Irish proverb, *An rud is fiú a dhéanamh, is fiú a dheanamh go maith*. If something is worth doing, it is worth doing well.

Maureen Murphy is a professor at Hofstra University and served as director of the Great Irish Famine Curriculum Project in New York State. She is a past president of the American Conference for Irish Studies.

# 1916:
# The Eoghan Rua
# Variations

Do threascair an saol is shéid an ghaoth mar smál
Alastrann, Caesar, 's an méid sin a bhí 'na bpáirt;
tá an Teamhair 'na féar, is féach an Traoi mar tá,
is na Sasanaigh féin do b'fhéidir go bhfaighidís bás.

Eoghan Rua O'Suilleabhain (1748–1782)

# PAUL MULDOON

1

On Easter Monday I was still en route
from Drumcondra to the GPO when I overheard a dispute
between a starch-shirt cuckoo
and a meadow pipit, the pipit singing even as it flew
between its perch on a wicker-covered carboy
and the nest it had improvised near a clump of gorse
from strands of linen spun by Henry Joy
and the mane of a stalking horse.
The cuckoo that had shouldered out the hoi polloi
showing not a hint of remorse.
Now the world's been brought low. The wind's heavy with soot.
Alexander and Caesar. All their retinue.
We've seen Tara buried in grass, Troy trampled underfoot.
The English? Their days are numbered, too.

2

Of the nine hundred Mauser rifles Erskine Childers and the boys
unloaded from the Asgard in Howth, most were deployed
to the Volunteers. Childers liked to trace "Howth" to its source
in the "hoarse Old Norse,"
the Vikings being among the first to beat their plowshares
into swords. On account of his opposition to it, the headstrong
O'Rahilly was simply not made aware
of the impending dingdong
even though the Viking blacksmiths on Mountjoy Square
had been going at it hammer and tongs.
The wind blows ash now the world's completely destroyed.
Alexander. Caesar. Each leading a mighty force.
Tara's overgrown. Look at the cut of Troy.
With the English, things may eventually take their course.

3

At Jacob's Biscuit Factory, Thomas MacDonagh sends up a flare
through the arrowroot-scented air.
On Stephen's Green, meanwhile, the English try to wrong-
foot us by launching a two-pronged
attack on our trenches. "The more we're spurned,"
Roger Casement once opined, "The more we're engrossed."
His submarine shaking from stem to stern
as it hugged the Kerry coast.
"The least stone," he went on, "The least stone in a cairn
is entitled to make one boast."
The whole world is laid waste. Cinders flying through the air.
Caesar and Alexander and their battle-throngs.
There's hardly a trace of Tara. Troy's barely there.
The English themselves will shortly be moving along.

4

Rather than adjourn to a gin palace for which so many yearned
Joseph Mary Plunkett has adjourned
to the GPO, where The O'Rahilly's now doing his utmost
to shove himself from pillar to post
in his newfound zeal to throw off the English yoke
and settle our old score.
On Sackville Street, a girl who seemed to be about to choke
has coughed up something from her very core.
She wipes her mouth on her jute cloak
and reloads her grandfather's four bore.
The sky is full of coal dust. The old order's overturned.
Caesar and Alexander. Their massed hosts.
Tara was burned. Troy was burned.
One of these days the English will give up the ghost.

5

I've watched Countess Markievicz striding through the oaks
where our aspirations turn out to be pigs in pokes.
This rifle was used against the Muslin sepoys in Cawnpore
before being turned on the Boers
but that its firing pin
is sticking is a sign of a more general morass
in which we founder. The thin
red line at Balaclava is testimony less to the officer class
than the rank and file. The din
of the sacking of Sackville Street. Looters. Broken glass.
The world laid waste. The wind heavy with smoke.
Alexander the Great. Great Caesar. Their assorted corps.
Tara is buried under grass. Even Troy's defenses broke.
In the case of the English, much the same lies in store.

## 6

MacDonagh's tapping out some rhythmic verse on a biscuit tin.
In Cawnpore, the sepoys were each sewn into a pig skin
before being hanged en masse.
On Stephens Green we got a whiff of that chlorine gas
with its distinctive pepper-pineapple smell.
The meadow pipit was shaking from stern to stem
as she pointed to the shell
of the cuckoo's egg she'd been condemned
to billet. As a dead horse's belly swells
it pushes a sniper out of his nest. Into murder and mayhem.
The wind all smut and smoor. The world spins
out of control. Alexander and Caesar. Their gangs under grass
like Tara of the Kings. Have you seen the shape Troy's in?
As for the English, that cup too will pass.

7

Daniel O'Connell. O'Donovan Rossa. Charles Stewart Parnell.
Patrick Pearse is sounding his own death knell
as that gob of phlegm
shines on the pavement in Sackville street. A little gem.
On Stephen's Green, one rare moment of mirth
comes with the daily ceasefire in which a keeper feeds the dank
ducks on their dank pond. For ourselves, there's a dearth
of humour. "Leave your jewels in the bank,"
the Countess told the girls. "The only thing worth
wearing's a revolver." It seems she shot one officer point-blank.
The whole world's foundering. A smoke trail tells
of the fates of Caesar, Alexander. Those who kissed their hems.
Tara's plowed under. Troy eventually fell.
Surely the English will get what's coming to them?

## 8

The dead horse's swollen belly has now so tightened its girth
it looks as if it might give birth
to a replica of itself. In an effort to outflank
us the English have banged out a tank
from the smoke-boxes of two locomotives. The men with a hand
on the tiller were so familiar with Tory Sound
they thought nothing of taking command
of the Asgard. To be renowned on Tory is to be world-renowned.
From a burst sandbag a skein of sand
winds as it's unwound.
The air tastes of grit. The world offers no safe berth.
Tsar Alexander. The Kaiser. Their serried ranks.
Tara is debased. You see how deep Troy lies beneath the earth.
The very English will sink as all those sank.

## 9

Those who can't afford a uniform may wear a blue armband
from which the meadow pipit filches a single strand
to bind its nest. The rest of us are bound
by honor alone. The English pound
the GPO while we ourselves meet brute strength with brute
determination. The pipit interweaves wondrous blue
and that workaday sandbag jute.
That the O'Rahilly was the last to know of the impending to-do
but first to execute
the plan of attack is ever so slightly skewed.
The world's topsy-turvy, though. This dust's the dust that fanned
Caesar and Alexander as each gained ground.
Tara's under pasture. At Troy, it's clear how things stand.
For the English, perhaps, their time will come around.

Commissioned by Glucksman Ireland House NYU
to mark the centennial of the 1916 Easter Rising.

Paul Muldoon won the Pulitzer Prize for Poetry in 2003.

Paul Muldoon reads his poem for the first time. ©NYU.

Clockwise from top left: Taoiseach Enda Kenny holds a copy of *Ireland's Allies: America and the 1916 Easter Rising*. Photo courtesy of James Higgins.

Novelist Peter Quinn, a longtime member of the Glucksman Ireland House, delivered a stirring address at the Irish Consulate General's commemoration of the Rising in Battery Park. Photo courtesy of James Higgins.

Actor Lisa Dwan and Fulbright Irish Language Scholar Anthony Duffy, with a reproduction of the Easter Proclamation. Photo courtesy of James Higgins.

# A Criminal Enterprise

## The Irish Crime Novel
## Comes of Age

# JOHN CONNOLLY

Warning: Readers of a sensitive disposition should note that
this story involves missing toes.

In 1999, I found myself an orphan.

Actually, that sounds wrong. It makes it appear as though I
were somehow scouring the streets looking for homeless urchins, which
isn't the case at all, and is the kind of misunderstanding that can land
a chap in all sorts of trouble. Rather, I personally became an orphan in
a very particular sense. In that year my first novel, *Every Dead Thing*,
was published in the United States, but by the time the book appeared
on shelves my editor had departed Simon & Schuster – possibly out
of shame – and my debut became, in publishing parlance, an 'orphan',
which meant that I, by extension, also became an orphan.

This is not an ideal situation for a fledgling writer. It means that the
person who might have been expected to fight one's corner when it
comes to marketing and general mollycoddling by the publisher, the
individual who loved one's book enough to acquire it in the first place,
is no more. Simon & Schuster did a fine job on the novel – I would not

be with them now, almost two decades later, had this not been the case – but I ended up going on something of a solo run in the United States to publicize the work.

Events were sparsely attended, when they were attended at all. This is not entirely surprising for a first-time novelist. After all, nobody yet knew who I was (most people still don't, and unless I somehow contrive to cure cancer this will almost certainly remain the case until the day I die), and wary punters could hardly be expected to give up an evening at home on the off chance that I might prove to be more entertaining than paring corns. Still, I can't pretend it wasn't disheartening, and so it was with a heavy heart that I approached the Black Orchid bookstore on New York's Upper East Side for what had been advertised as an 'informal signing.' This meant that I wasn't expected to make a speech or declaim sections of my deathless prose, but merely sign stock and leave as quickly as possible with the least possible offense given – or taken, as the bookseller couldn't be blamed if no punters toddled along to buy a book since I hadn't promised the full dog-and-pony show.

It was a Friday afternoon, which is hardly primetime for book signings, and consequently the greeting from the store's owners was more effusive than I deserved. I suspect they may have felt a bit sorry for me, which made three of us.

But we were not alone.

Seated on a folding chair just inside the front door was a big man who had clearly suffered some recent catastrophic injury to his left foot, which was encased in the kind of protective covering usually associated with fragile works of ancient art, or unstable explosives.

I was, I confess, immediately wary. I had already learned that certain independent stores, once they gain a sufficient patina of age, often acquire That Customer: the guy – and it's usually a male – who has made himself as essential a fixture as the shelves and carpets, so much so that he even has his own chair surrounded by a virtual exclusion zone, especially when he happens to be *in situ*, which is most of the time.

In the absence of a chair, he will lean on the counter and pass many a happy hour discoursing on the issues of the day with anyone foolish enough to stand still long enough to attract his attention. You've met him. We all have. If you haven't, then you are he. To complicate matters, the owners were now trying to introduce me to what was clearly a prime specimen, perhaps in the hope that I might take him off their hands by adopting him.

In the end, good manners triumphed over common sense. After all, what was one to do but say hello?

The gentleman's name was Joe Long, born in Chelsea to Irish parents, and he was a steadfast customer of the store. He had recently been forced to endure the amputation of part of his left foot, including a number of toes, and was recuperating on the orders of his physician. This meant, as he informed me without even a glimmer of concern for my sensitivities, that he had no excuse available when he was asked by the Black Orchid to rise from his sick bed in order to shake the hand of a young Irish writer (since no one else was likely to make an appearance), and perhaps buy a copy of the book to make the young Irish writer feel wanted.

So he wasn't That Customer, but something far worse: he was The Guy With Nothing Better To Do. This, it seemed, was destined to be my fan base: Irish-American invalids vulnerable to emotional blackmail.

But hey, a sale is a sale.

Unfortunately, it wasn't going to be that easy. Joe handed me twenty dollars and told me to go buy a six-pack of beer for everyone to share. Now I may have been a neophyte author, but it seemed to me unlikely that this was the done thing when a novelist came to visit a bookstore. Who knew, though? Perhaps Stephen King, when he was starting out, ran the odd errand for codgers in return for the purchase of a copy of *Carrie*. Donna Tartt might have agreed to watch someone's car on condition that a sale of *The Secret History* followed. Frankly, I wasn't intimate with enough writers to be able to say for certain either way.

Reader, I went out and bought the beer. I even returned with the correct change. Shortly thereafter, a lady arrived to buy a book – although not one of mine, blast her. She moved slowly and painfully, aided by a cane. It emerged that she had injured herself by falling down an elevator shaft. I had never before met anyone who claimed to have fallen down an elevator shaft. Even Joe, who worked for an elevator company, had never met anyone who had fallen down an elevator shaft, or not the way this woman appeared to have. According to her version of events, the elevator doors opened, she stepped in, and immediately took the express route down owing to the absence of an actual elevator.

It was that kind of afternoon.

Out of unlikely encounters notable developments may emerge. It would not be an exaggeration to say that the history of Irish crime writing would be very different had Joe Long not limped his way to Black Orchid that day, or had I done the sensible thing and told him to buy his own beer, goddammit.

Joe and I stayed in touch, and eventually became friends. Some years later, he decided to take a Master's in Irish and Irish-American Studies at NYU, and became part of the first intake for that degree in 2007. By then Joe Long probably knew as much about Irish crime writing as anyone in the United States, and had become a proselytizer for a form of literature that had only recently gained a foothold in its native country.

After almost a century of neglect, Irish genre fiction was resurgent. Arguably, this process had commenced back in 1982 with the publication of Maeve Binchy's *Light A Penny Candle*, which was among the first novels to suggest Irish writing might be able to achieve a degree of commercial success to match its critical acclaim. It was women's contemporary fiction, with Binchy at the forefront, that initially attracted the attention of British and American publishers to Irish popular literature, but it took a little longer for other genres to reap the benefits, crime fiction among them.

Irish writers had explored the possibilities of the crime genre throughout the twentieth century, but many had been forgotten,

Joe Long, after earning his master's degree. ©NYU.

enjoyed only limited success, or were co-opted as British by our friends across the Irish Sea – but only the successes; the failures, you may not be entirely shocked to learn, remained Irish to the core. Of the former, the hugely prolific Golden Age crime novelist Freeman Wills Crofts was born in Dublin, and the British Poet Laureate Cecil Day-Lewis, who wrote mysteries under the pseudonym Nicholas Blake, came from Ballintubbert, County Laois. By the 1990s, writers as varied as Eugene McEldowney, Paul Charles, Ken Bruen, and Colin Bateman had been added to the list, and more would follow, but there remained, I think, a certain ambivalence about native crime writing among Irish critics and in Irish academic circles, an equivocation that extended to all home-produced genre fiction.

Unlike in Britain and the United States, genre writing had yet to enjoy very much serious critical consideration in Ireland, and was regarded, in the main, as strictly second-division stuff. I can still recall the difficulties experienced by Professor Ian Campbell Ross in convincing the relevant authorities in Trinity College Dublin that crime fiction was worthy of study as part of the university's offerings in modern English literature. He persevered, thankfully, and a course in the subject was introduced in the early 1990s, to which I was lucky enough to be accepted, but one could hear the sniffs of academic disapproval all the way from Grafton Street.

The changes since then have been rapid. Trinity College's MPhil in Popular Literature – the first of its kind to be offered anywhere in the world – is now in its second decade. Horror, speculative fiction, and romance are taught in the university alongside Modernist poets and the greats of nineteenth-century fiction, and similar courses are available in other Irish third-level institutions, but it was the study of crime fiction that led the way. The genre, in its Irish incarnation, now enjoys significant commercial success both at home and abroad – although, interestingly, in a predominantly female form: women dominate the field, a turn of events which should provide academic essayists with a steady stream of income for years to come.

NYU has been integral to this process. When Joe Long shared his passion for Irish crime writing with his fellow MA students – and with Professor John Waters – it resulted in my being invited to speak to the class about Ireland's relationship with the genre. Following that visit, and with the active support of NYU, a steady stream of Irish crime writers began to make their way to Glucksman Ireland House for seminars, book launches, and symposia. In 2013, the circle begun by Ian Ross back in 1991 was completed when Trinity College and NYU came together to host, on TCD's campus, the largest crime fiction festival ever held in Ireland.

It's a funny thing about the Irish (and it may be to do with a sense of post-colonial inadequacy), but we often require our artists, writers, and musicians to receive validation from abroad before we are content to accept that their creative efforts may have genuine merit. So while the generosity and enthusiasm of NYU, and particularly the staff at Glucksman Ireland House, have contributed enormously to bringing Irish crime fiction to greater international attention, this support has also helped to fasten the genre's reputation in its native land. Thus it is that, for many Irish crime writers, the mention of Glucksman Ireland House evokes a sense of gratitude and affection entirely out of proportion to the actual time spent inside its walls. NYU had faith in us when it mattered, and we won't forget it.

All because an Irish-American with a bum foot decided not to stay home one day.

All for the price of a six-pack of beer.

John Connolly is the author of the Charlie Parker and Samuel Johnson series of novels, among other works.

# Coming of Age

## A New Generation
## Makes its Mark

# RAY O'HANLON

Irish America is precisely that.

Something Irish, something American.

And while history suggests that the pairing is a natural fit, there has always been an element of competition, push and pull, sometimes outright conflict as one side goes about influencing, and sometimes changing, the other.

This latter aspect was especially evident in the last quarter-century, a time of profound change in Ireland, and therefore in Irish America. Twenty-five years ago, many newly arrived Irish immigrants were on their way to adding a hyphen to their identity, thanks to congressional legislation that gave birth to visa programs named for the lawmakers who sponsored them: Donnelly, Berman, Morrison and Schumer. The island they had left behind, most of them in the 1980s, was a youthful place in demographic terms, but old hat in terms of economic opportunity.

These new Irish Americans would, as their ancestors always had, cast an eye back to their point of origin. But, over time, they would see something that their forebears had not: an Ireland beginning to catch up to the rest of Europe and their new home, America, in economic and social aspirations, norms and standards.

This was an entirely new type of emigration/immigration, one in which old certainties were jettisoned and replaced by potentially unsettling choices, not least a return to Ireland for more than a vacation. The westward movement of the 1980s also led to a fault line in immigrant life: On one side of the line were green card holders, on the other were those who had not been so fortunate in the various visa lotteries. So there were two kinds of Irish immigrants: Those with required paperwork, and those without.

Irish America would hear from both.

The undocumented would loudly protest their exclusion from an America that had started to close its doors to the Irish with the 1965 Immigration and Nationality Act.

The emergence of the Irish Immigration Reform Movement (IIRM) was an early indicator that many of the newcomers were unwilling to be quietly looked after by their Irish American kith and kin.

The undocumented wanted to be legal, not only due to the labors and sacrifices of their Irish American cousins over the centuries, but also because of who they were, and the opportunities in life they had been raised to expect.

The IIRM's loud public protests would draw attention from America's mainstream media and spark a revival in Irish-American journalism with the birth of the *Irish Voice* newspaper in 1987 and the subsequent rejuvenation of the *Irish Echo*, which had been Irish America's primary sounding board since the end of the 1920s.

The newcomers knew media, too. They could lure it like a moth to a flame.

The IIRM would spark stories in big city newspapers and reports on national television networks.

But the energy of the new Irish, legal and otherwise, was hardly confined to a single issue, important though immigration reform was.

It soon became apparent that the new Irish had a range of expectations, world views, and hopes that seemed utterly alien to an older generation of immigrants and to many American-born Irish. But times were changing, and the new Irish were among those advocating for change, forcing change, and doing so in a way that profoundly affected not just Irish America, but Ireland as well.

Young immigrants helped to found the Irish Lesbian and Gay Organization (ILGO) in New York to advocate for tolerance and inclusion, demanding a place for themselves in the greatest expression of Irish identity in the world – the St. Patrick's Day Parade in New York. Through their activism and persistence, ILGO and offspring organizations like the Lavender and Green Alliance were harbingers of profound change in Ireland – from a distance of 3,000 miles – and within Irish America.

The Irish Lesbian and Gay Organization protested New York's St. Patrick's Day Parade beginning in the early 1990s in an effort to allow a gay organization to march behind its own banner. Photo courtesy of the Archives of Irish America, Bobst Library, New York University.

In 1993, just a few years after ILGO was founded, Ireland decriminalized same-sex relations. That same year, 230 ILGO members were arrested on Fifth Avenue on St. Patrick's Day as they protested their exclusion from the parade.

Few would have predicted any of this even a decade earlier. But then again, the pace of change in Irish America didn't leave much time for peering into the future. Change was so dramatic in the 1990s that it was completely unpredictable.

Who would have dared to envision what unfolded as the new Irish in America came of age?

An American president, with combined Irish and Irish-American support, intervened in the Troubles in Northern Ireland. And the Troubles came to an end.

Irish Americans, spurred on by new arrivals from across the Atlantic, took greater control of their own story with books, films, and music. The Great Hunger, that end of days for old Ireland and moment of birth for modern Irish America, became the subject of new scholarship and research thanks to the expanding field of Irish Studies.

The Celtic Tiger confused and amused. The new Irish Americans found themselves explaining why they had left an Ireland that suddenly seemed to be awash in money. Some were lured back across the Atlantic. And some would not like what they found and would head west again. It surely was unpredictable, as was the cultural revival of Irish America that the newcomers helped to inspire.

Young Irish immigrants like Helena Mulkerns and Emer Martin achieved artistic success and notice in New York, no small achievement, in the 1990s.

Colum McCann, an immigrant from Dublin, would write about people back 'home' and his adopted American neighbors, of the former with knowledge aforethought, of the latter with knowledge gleaned from keenly observing the inhabitants of his new place. Enniscorthy-born Colm Tóibín found a new home and inspiration in New York in the 1990s. The *New York Times* would say that his novels were all about searching for home. And now that could equally be Brooklyn or Wexford.

Meanwhile, the new Irish Americans went about their lives and their business as others had before them, embracing their hyphenated identity while becoming, perhaps to their surprise, more American than they had ever imagined. They transformed aging urban neighborhoods – Woodside and Woodlawn, Dorchester, Upper Darby, Tinley Park – and then, as time passed and an immigrant generation produced the next first generation, they began to scatter to the promised land of suburbia.

They made their mark not only in traditional industries such as hospitality and construction, but as entrepreneurs, writers and artists, and white-collar professionals. They were as familiar with technology in a new building as they were with topping it off.

The Irish who arrived in America in the early 1990s are now in their middle years – the prime of life. Many have had children of their own, American by birth, and while so much about them was new and different in 1993, they now find themselves living out a version of a traditional narrative, the Irish immigrant story.

But while the outline may be familiar, the specifics surely are very different. And those differences have created nothing less than a transatlantic cultural revolution that has enriched the Irish experience wherever green is worn.

Ray O'Hanlon is editor of the *Irish Echo* and author of *The New Irish Americans*.

# Bridging the
# Transatlantic Gap

# PATRICIA HARTY

In 1985, Niall O'Dowd and I decided to publish a magazine, *Irish America*. All these years later, it's clear to see that that we were on the verge of something new, exciting and tumultuous, both in Irish-American life and in publishing. But that was not so evident at the time. We've gone through some rough patches, but we have survived. Just as the Irish-American experience has changed over the last quarter-century, the publishing industry has evolved as well, bringing us online with www.irishamerica.com. I'll confess that while I like the convenience of the web and social media, I prefer print magazines, and we still do a print issue.

The joy for me is turning the page. A well-put-together magazine is a piece of art. I love matching word to photos, working with writers, designers, copyediting, proofreading, and type. I love type – I'm mad about kerning the space between letters.

Before I left home for the States, I'd studied painting and drawing at night school at Limerick School of Art and Design. After landing in the Bronx, USA, I studied at Lehman College and later, after moving to Manhattan, took classes at the School of Visual Arts. Like many

Irish who would arrive in waves after me in the late 1980s, I didn't have a green card. I supported myself by waitressing, and managed to head over to a design studio to learn how to put mechanicals together and study the elements of design with a wonderful teacher, Annette Sullivan.

I worked for a small graphics company owned by Frank Quinn. I was dating his nephew, Bobby, and that was my toe, so to speak, in the door. It was 1976.

I had excellent typing skills thanks to nuns who blacked the keys on manual typewriters and had us practice relentlessly while concentrating on a mock-up of the keyboard posted on the blackboard.

But the art of typesetting proved tricky: those early Compugraphic phototypesetting machines were still relatively new, and the one I used had no previewer. There were certain codes that you had to put in for italics or bold type, or to change to a different typeface.

So, this is a long way of saying that when I moved to San Francisco in 1979 and met Niall O'Dowd, I knew how to produce his newspaper.

My brother Desi picked me up at the airport and took me to the Blarney Stone Bar on Geary Street. Niall blustered in with a bunch of newspapers under his arm – he had just come from the printers with the first copies of *The Irishman*, named, of course, in honor of the United Irishmen who launched the rebellion of 1798.

I wasn't too impressed with the paper's design and soon I was putting my graphic art and typesetting skills to work on improving the layout, and at the same time, gaining some valuable knowledge about the Irish in America.

I knew the story of earlier generations of Irish immigrants was a rich one because I'd taken a three-month bus trip around the country. Everywhere I went I saw signs that other Irish had been here before me. There was the Irish Bayou in New Orleans, O'Neill, Nebraska, and Dublin, Ohio, and I was curious to know more about how those signs and place names came to be.

They didn't tell us about the Irish in America when we were growing up in Ireland. We learned about the coffin ships that took them across the Atlantic during the blight times, but not what happened to them here.

Sean McGeever's history pieces for *The Irishman* were an education. He wrote on the Copper Kings of Montana, and the Irish who worked on the railroads. And I began to explore on my own. I visited the Mission Dolores graveyard where so many Irish, some of them young men lured by the gold rush, are buried. Their headstones almost always list their home counties.

When Niall and I moved to New York in 1985 to start *Irish America* magazine, I continued to learn from people like Dennis Clark, Pete Hamill, Eoin McKiernan, Peter Quinn, Mary Pat Kelly and William D. Griffin, whose book, *The Irish American: The Immigrant Experience*, became my bible. Unlike today, there weren't too many books about the Irish then – remember, this was the same time Irish writers often were classified as 'British' and Ireland's movies were filed under 'UK' in the video stores.

So when Glucksman Ireland House opened right on my own doorstep in Manhattan in 1993, it was as if the cavalry had arrived. Great writers, Irish and American, commentators, historians, economists and politicians flocked through its doors, and I got to meet them all. I interviewed Seamus Heaney just steps away in Washington Square Park, and just months after he had won the Nobel Prize for Literature.

The Irish were on the rise, and they had a home to call their own – a townhouse on Washington Square Mews, welcoming and warm, a place where the stories of Ireland are treasured.

Under Robert Scally, the wise inaugural director, and later Joe Lee, Glucksman Ireland House became a place where hope and history rhyme; a place that bridges the gap between Irish and Irish America, and the home of one of the finest Irish Studies programs in the world.

It is a place where the past is not lost. It preserves our story, the story of a people, many of whom were from rural areas and had never been higher than the local hill, built skyscrapers – a man named Louis Sullivan, son of immigrants, would become known as the 'father of skyscrapers' – and went hundreds of feet into the earth to dig the water tunnels that served the nation's largest city. They built the canals – all 363 miles of the Erie Canal, which connected the Great Lakes to the Hudson River. And they died in the swamps of New Orleans, their lives worth less than the slaves who worked along the banks.

They died young in crowded tenements. A cholera epidemic in Boston took away Patrick Kennedy, native of County Wexford, in 1858, leaving behind a widow, Bridget, to raise four children on her own – there would have been five, but one child, named John, died of the same disease that killed her husband.

Bridget Kennedy was just one of countless women who kept their families together in the face of personal tragedy and society's indifference. She worked hard, ran a little stationary shop on the wharf, and lived to see her son P.J., who left school at 14 to help his mother and sisters in the shop, become a successful businessman and politician. She lived to see the birth of her grandson Joseph Patrick 'Joe' Kennedy in September, 1888, just a couple of months before she died. Could she ever have dreamed that Joe's son, John, named after her own dead son, would be become president of the United States?

My abiding memory of a lunch at NYU's Bobst Library announcing plans for the creation of Glucksman Ireland House is riding up in the elevator with John Kennedy, Jr., Bridget and Patrick Kennedy's great great-grandson. Some of the light went out of Irish America in 1999 when John's plane crashed into the Atlantic – that 'veil of tears,' the final resting place of so many other Irish who died fleeing starvation in Ireland in the 1840s. We remember them, but we think of another great Irish woman, the labor leader Mary 'Mother' Jones who said, 'Pray for the dead but take care of the living.' And we take joy in those who did

John F. Kennedy greets Taoiseach Charles Haughey as Loretta Brennan Glucksman looks on during a luncheon announcing the creation of the House. ©NYU.

make it – Henry Ford, the great American industrialist, whose father came over on a sailing ship in 1847 and is said to have jumped overboard and swum ashore to escape the cholera-infested ship being held in quarantine. We take heart in knowing their courage and determination. The students who go through the doors of Glucksman Ireland House will know their story. And they will take it to their heart and perhaps they too, in times of trouble, will be reminded that – as Pete Hamill says – you just have to 'keep on keeping on.'

For the vision and generosity of Loretta Brennan Glucksman and her husband Lewis Glucksman, who have done so much to keep the story of the Irish in America alive, we give thanks.

Patricia Harty is the editor of *Irish America* magazine.

# A Student's Long Journey Home

Of Irish writing, culture, scholarship,
An answer given to the famine ship,
A feis, a court of poetry, a seisiún,
Academy and legacy, a boon.

Seamus Heaney

# ELLEN O'BRIEN KELLY

To step inside 1 Washington Mews – the building I would come to know dearly as 'the House' – is to put oneself within its warm embrace: a pulsing epicenter of grace, hospitality, charm, wit, culture, and supreme intellect. Where the kettle was always on, and Barry's tea was found in its cupboards … the books, the artifacts, the voices – instantly familiar accents that had long left my ear – each of these things filled me in places I'd unwittingly abandoned.

It was the Irish language I was after at first. I hadn't been able to reconcile facts gleaned from census records with the memory of such hushed utterances as 'They took our language away.' Each of my grandparents, emigrants in the late 1920s, had arrived in New York City with two languages in tow – their native Irish, and English. Why had I never heard Irish spoken? Still more curious was the seemingly bold entry, 'Irish Free State,' where other immigrants had recorded, simply, 'Ireland.' Intrigued, I wondered what, if any, significance this phrase had for them. More so, how had their bilingualism become akin to something whispered, a seeming casualty of their Irishness? Bereft with the knowledge of their histories long buried, I was suddenly struck with a longing to know more.

A heritage rooted in Irish-American Catholicism had not escaped me. Irish music was played; and we were taught Irish step and set dancing. The tunes so familiar I would one day sing the Clancy Brothers' 'Weile Waile' on a high school bus trip. We ate soda bread and drank tea; we were mad for blood pudding. It took years before my mother would add garlic to a recipe, and, to be sure, it came in powder form! Gatherings were integral to the family's social fabric: christenings, communions, weddings, and yes, wakes. And there was always the chat reflecting the two places my relatives occupied: JFK, the Pope, LBJ, MLK Jr., and Bobby; Reagan, Thatcher, the Troubles, Bernadette, and Bobby. This cultural immersion was not experienced as a forced ideology, but rather as an intrinsic ownership of an identity to which they felt strongly connected, and, I might add, proud.

So proud, in fact, that St. Patrick's Day seemed as high a holy day as Christmas. Fondly I recall going downtown with my father to meet my grandmother and her band of Hibernians with whom we'd 'march up the avenue.' Her delight as she shouted, 'England! Get out of Ireland!' and 'Up Cork!' imbued me with a sense of belonging to this land that summoned such fervent spirit. It was this grandmother with whom I would first go to Ireland. Eleven years of age and flown across an ocean – it was a memory both instantly and eternally seared. Whether it was the bevy of new clothes, the Aer Lingus flight through the night, or to behold from the early morning sky the most glorious sea of green fields I had ever laid eyes upon, the sense of having arrived home was profound. And it was this same grandmother who seemed to be calling me home again, to 'the House' where her language was no longer whispered, but, rather elevated: the stuff of scholars.

Native speaker and teacher Pádraig Ó Cearúil and his Irish language class brought me to the House's doorstep. Once inside there was no turning back. Not only had I found 'the House' where the Irish language was spoken, studied, and celebrated, I would soon discover its graduate program dedicated to scholarly, artistic, and cultural achievement. With

© NYU.

children engaged in their undergraduate careers, I decided to pursue the Glucksman Ireland House Master of Arts program. A premiere center of Irish and Irish American studies, 1 Washington Mews would become my Rock of Cashel, my Hill of Tara, my Blarney Stone: where legend and history commingle, where memory and trope are challenged, where intellect and heart coincide.

I was somewhat intimidated at the start, as it had been some time since my undergraduate days, but my professors quickly revealed themselves as engaging and, importantly, approachable. Their keen intellects seemed to extend easily beyond each professor's distinct expertise. In a two-and-a-half-hour weekly lecture, Professor John Waters explored historiography, cartography, poetry, literature, and music all without a single reference to notes. This teaching style of seemingly unscripted brilliance proved true in each of my courses. Professor Joe Lee's lecture ran the gamut of modern Irish and Irish-American history, from *An Gorta Mór* to the Irish Land Act, from Gladstone, Home Rule, and Redmond to the Easter Rising, Devoy, Pearse, and de Valera, or as Professor Lee would say, 'Dev.' Professor Lee's lectures evaluated seminal moments of Irish history within the context of a nineteenth- and twentieth-century European theater in its entirety. With Professor Lee you entered a living history: a baptism by a world-class academic whose heart was as much at the forefront of his lecture as his brilliant mind.

With Professor Mick Moloney, the Irish music and dance of my childhood became a course of study through which cultural identity was thoroughly and enthusiastically examined. Professor Moloney's dissertation, 'Irish Music in America,' provided me with a wholly new appreciation for the steps and tunes my parents had so cherished. I pored over its pages, as well as the works of other scholars in which detailed and rich research was applied to the study of Irish and Irish-American music. And The Chieftains – a staple on my parents' turntable – became a subject of research in which I made a case for Paddy Moloney's impact upon the globalization of Irish music. In a Mick Moloney lecture, music, culture, history and folklore commingled much like it would in a ballad. And I was always left wanting more.

Answers soon materialized. With every class and each assigned reading, torrents of information filled my mind. Books about Irish history and culture, as well as Post-its galore, occupied every nook and cranny of my home. From Professor Marion Casey's highly regarded research on New York's Irish, as well as her engaging and informative lectures, I came to know my parents and grandparents through an academic lens, worthy of historical analysis and insight. Academia has regarded this specific community of 1920s emigrants and first-generation Irish Americans as the Mott Haven Irish. In our home, however, their Bronx neighborhood was warmly known as St. Luke's. And what I came to know as a student of Irish studies, I could testify to first-hand: this community embraced its Irish ethnicity organically, and passed on its unique sense of Irishness to children and grandchildren, and in particular to me, through music.

The research Professor Casey advised me to undertake with regard to this community enabled me to better understand my deceased grandparents' census entry, 'Irish Free State.' Without knowing their specific politics in that volatile period in Ireland, it is safe to surmise my grandparents arrived in New York City with perhaps a stronger sense of Irish national identity than their own grandparents would have known. This community of immigrants was among the first to embrace its culture as distinctive and worthy of celebration. That the Mott Haven Irish played the music, danced the sets, sang the songs, joined the county associations and marched in its most celebrated parade bespoke a love of country no longer lost on me, but cherished anew. As participants of a Gaelic revival, my grandparents and parents bequeathed to their descendants – my siblings and our children – the transmission of its culture evidenced by our participation in the fields of music, dance, theater, film, literature, government, and history. And the awareness of this pronounced legacy filled me in those places I feared had been abandoned.

This is the magic that is Glucksman Ireland House. Each of its professors unearths and exacts from its students what often times presents as an intangible connection to Ireland and Irish America. Through their passion for Irish and Irish-American studies, students come to understand what one's Irishness might mean. And Miriam Nyhan Grey captures the essence of this magic brilliantly, changing the intangible to tangible almost daily. Dr. Grey epitomizes the warmth and intellect that is Glucksman Ireland House, as do each of the House's gifted scholars.

It had been a while since I marched the avenue on St. Patrick's Day. But the House and its Irish heartbeat managed, yet again, to connect me to those hearts I've loved and lost throughout the years. This year, St. Patrick's Day found me on 5th Avenue, not with my grandmother but instead behind Glucksman Ireland House's benefactor and visionary, Loretta Brennan Glucksman, the parade's Grand Marshal. Alongside me were a new band of Hibernians: a community of alumni, graduate and undergraduate students alike, each of whom found their way to the House much like myself. And each of whom, like me, found 'Of Irish writing, culture, scholarship / An answer given to the famine ship / A feis, a court of poetry, a seisiún / Academy and legacy, a boon' at that most welcoming of all addresses, 1 Washington Mews.

Ellen O'Brien Kelly's documentary film, *From Ballinakill to Booton: Irish Traditional Music in New Jersey,* has been shown in several cultural festivals and conferences.

# The
# Irish-American Mews
# and Oral History

# MIRIAM NYHAN GREY

Glucksman Ireland House is the product of a mixed marriage – like myself, Cork and Laois. Our Irish-American and Jewish-American founders set a tone just by their being. Freed of the constraints that limited the ambitions of their Irish, Catholic and Jewish antecedents, New York and New York University opened up new vistas in the 1990s, especially in terms of how to preserve the fragments of the lives of migrants and their descendants through the medium of oral history.

It is worth remembering that the Glucksmans conceived of Ireland House in a time when Irish identity was fraught with borders and bombs. When being gay in Ireland made one a criminal and an Irish divorce was an impossibility. And at a time when being Irish meant being white and Catholic, almost to a man; pun intended.

From the vantage point of April 1993, no one could foresee that peace could or would soon come to the island of Ireland, especially when the Shankill Road bombing dominated the headlines in October of that year. Or that the attack on the World Trade Center which took place exactly two months prior to the opening of Ireland House was merely a prelude to a new world order; one in which identity would be misappropriated

Photo courtesy of James Higgins.

to underscore the differences, instead of the universalities, in the human experience.

The oral histories housed at New York University's Archives of Irish America provide us with a rich resource through which we can excavate the past. Hours of narrative, representing over 350 voices, tell us a great deal about the human experience. We interrogate what it means to be Irish and American; to be Irish American or American Irish. We explore why people think of themselves as Irish when they have other ethnicities or motifs of identify from which to choose. Embedded in the collection are abundant insights into the texture of lived experiences. Successes and failures. Tears and triumphs.

In 2006, I came to NYU on a doctoral exchange scholarship from Italy's European University Institute to conduct oral histories and to spend some time at an institution enriched by the inimitable Joe Lee. I did complete my studies in the Florentine hills but I have not left New York for any significant amount of time since then and the collection of oral histories has been a significant part of my contribution to Glucksman Ireland House since my arrival. It is, indeed, a labor of love. Not that long ago we captured the memories of a nonagenarian whose father had lived through Ireland's famine of the 1840s. What a humbling experience it was to confront the breadth of history in that way. Similarly sobering are the reflections of a 1950s adoptee from Ireland – born in the mother and baby home made famous through the pages of *The Lost Child of Philomena Lee* and on screen in *Philomena* – which complicate our interpretations of the history of transatlantic adoptions.

Savage PTSD-infused sensory reminiscences permeate the narrative of an artist who, as he worked on Battery Park's Irish Hunger Memorial, bore witness to another attack on the World Trade Center on a beautiful September morning in 2001. On another occasion, I sat with a Pentagon employee who had a rich family history as a Montanan of Irish descent. As he descended an escalator in the Pentagon on 9/11 the nose of a jet violently breached the building and knocked him off his feet, derailing his habitual Starbucks run.

The richness of Irish culture and its global footprint are laid bare in the interview with a choreographer whose artistic contribution forever changed a genre, way back in 1994 when Glucksman Ireland House was just a year old. The memories of at least two American-born children who were sent to Ireland for economic reasons in the 1940s allow us to understand that the struggles of some immigrants persisted long after the Great Depression had ended.

I asked one interviewee for her first memory. She could not think of one but instead shared her husband's earliest recollection of waking up as a young child in the late 1930s or early 1940s to a member of the Klu Klux Klan, in full regalia, staring in the window at him. Word was out in the small southern town where they had relocated that Catholics had moved in. Fresh meat. This experience seemed so removed from her own childhood in mid twentieth-century Mayo.

One summer, while I was in Ireland, I interviewed a man who was born on a barge on the Hudson River who didn't think that this feature of his birth was particularly notable. He would spend his life working close to water, engaged in maritime pursuits between New York and my home town of Arklow. Then there are the reflections of Tommy, who was passing the Dakota apartment building in December 1980 as Mark Chapman was being detained and John Lennon lay dying nearby. Tommy had recognized the sound of gunfire and expressed regret at not having a tape recorder with him at the time to capture the sounds of the chaos of that historic moment. Sometimes we do recognize when we are on the sidelines of history.

The archive houses the emotional response of an Irish American who was interviewed days after the election of President Barack Obama in 2008 and who recognized what that historic milestone did to uplift African Americans. She indicated an empathy, which I sensed was something new for her, based on how the election of John F. Kennedy in 1960 had been heralded in her Queens home. As one might anticipate in a collection of interviews with Irish Americans, there are many personal reflections about Kennedy's assassination on November 22, 1963. So many still remember where they were when the terrible news from Dallas broke on that Friday afternoon, and their reminiscences of Kennedy's state funeral in Washington – the horse-drawn caisson, the funeral Mass said by Boston's archbishop, Cardinal Richard Cushing, the lighting of an eternal flame on a hillside in Arlington National Cemetery – were equally vivid all these years later. The pain, the senselessness of it all, was also evident. Kennedy's murder represented an affront to everything the Irish celebrated as American. He was one of their own.

We have also recorded an interview with a man who fully embraced being Irish without having, I am pretty certain, any Irish ancestry. When he died, communities in Irish New York and in Ireland were devastated by his passing after a short illness. But who am I to judge if he was not, as I suspect, genetically Irish at all? And more to the point, why would I? Glucksman Ireland House partly derived from the vision of a man who was not of Irish lineage. Lew Glucksman's passion for things Irish long pre-dated his Irish-American muse, Loretta Brennan Glucksman, the granddaughter of four Irish immigrants. Engagements with Ireland,

Irish America and the global Irish diaspora have never been defined or essentialized by claims of genetic, hereditary or cultural ownership at Washington Mews. Nor will they be. How can they be in a city like New York and on a campus whose home is Greenwich Village?

Ireland has changed considerably since Glucksman Ireland House opened its doors in 1993. The ways by which the Irish are identified and how they self-identify have been redefined fundamentally. The highest political office in Ireland is occupied by an openly gay man who is the son of an Indian immigrant. He and his partner marched in the 257th St. Patrick's Day Parade behind only the fifth woman to lead New York's pinnacle of ethnic celebration. That woman was, of course, our own Loretta Brennan Glucksman.

In his 2009 interview for the Archives of Irish America, the celebrated writer Pete Hamill was asked if he defined himself as a New Yorker:

> Yeah, I'm a New Yorker. Which means, that I'm proudly and profoundly Irish-American, but I'm also Jewish-American. I'm African-American. I'm Chinese-American. I'm very much Mexican-American... So New York is an odd case ... [but] I feel comfortable there. I'm not wary, I don't feel menace. I feel, this is my place to live.

Pete's outlook, shaped in Brooklyn by two Belfast-born immigrants, could be used as a blueprint for how we view identity at New York University. How we confront and celebrate and then how we interrogate and document the diversity of the Irish experience will continue to mold the research and teaching agenda of Glucksman Ireland House for many years to come.

Oh, and in the meantime, we'll just keep on interviewing.

Miriam Nyhan Grey is the associate director of Glucksman Ireland House and director of graduate studies.

# An Enduring Connection

## Ties that Bind Will Survive the Digital Age

Like oil lamps, we put them out the back—
of our houses, of our minds. We had lights
better than, newer than and then
a time came, this time and now
we need them.

Eavan Boland, *The Emigrant Irish*

# DANIEL MULHALL

Until I arrived in Washington in August 2017, my experience of America and of Irish America was limited to a summer spent as a J1 student in Kansas City in 1974. I had, of course, read a great deal about American history and politics. Colleagues at the Department of Foreign Affairs had often spoken about what a special privilege it is to serve as an Irish diplomat in the United States. My experience of representing Ireland here has more than lived up to expectations.

It is a large part of my work as ambassador to understand and engage with our diaspora in the United States. It is not a task to be taken for granted, for there is no guarantee that people of Irish descent in America will choose to identify with their ancestral homeland. So there is a huge incentive for us to encourage continued Irish-American interest in Ireland, including through the fostering of Irish Studies in America.

First, though, it is important to understand why Irish America has remained so attached to Ireland, many decades after the era of mass migration came to an end. It surely has something to do with how the Irish community reorganized itself in the United States as hundreds of thousands arrived during the Great Famine and its aftermath. They

Daniel and Greta Mulhall visit Glucksman Ireland House in fall 2017 and meet faculty, staff and Loretta Brennan Glucksman and Ted Smyth, chair and president of the Advisory Board respectively. © NYU.

generated a sense of community and solidarity, a rural people who found themselves in the great cities of America, and were armed with a strong sense of grievance against British rule in Ireland. The hostility of nativist movements in America only deepened their sense of community cohesion.

The enduring connection between Ireland and America was a critical factor in the planning and execution of the Easter Rising in 1916. The publication of *Ireland's Allies: America and the Easter Rising*, edited by Miriam Nyhan Grey of Glucksman Ireland House, reminded us that, as former Glucksman Ireland House director Joe Lee put it, 'No Irish America, no New York, no Easter Rising. Simple as that.'

Even when the Irish Free State was established in 1922, Irish Americans continued to follow and engage with events across the Atlantic. That continued interest no doubt derived from Irish America's sense that Irish independence was incomplete. It was not dimmed when Ireland remained neutral during the Second World War and maintained that neutrality in the post-war world, declining to join the North Atlantic Treaty Organization when it was formed in 1949. Over the decades, Irish diplomats kept up contact with key Irish-American organizations and influencers – in the 1950s in order to enlist their support in anti-partition efforts, and from the 1970s onwards to encourage support for the Irish Government's pursuit of peace and reconciliation in Northern Ireland.

In more recent times, the backing of the global Irish was vital as Ireland battled the adversities of the Great Recession. The success of the Global Irish Economic Forum (GIEF) which first met in September 2009, and The Gathering of 2013 encouraged a more strategic approach to diaspora engagement, reflected in the government's global Irish policy and in the funding provided to Irish organizations around the world through the Department of Foreign Affairs and Trade's Emigrant Support Programme. The centenary of the Easter Rising was marked with pride and enthusiasm across the United States, which pointed to an enduring affection for, and interest in, Irish heritage.

But what of our interactions with Irish America as we enter into the second century of Irish independence? How to connect an evolving Irish community in America with a transformed Ireland? While many things have changed on both sides of the Atlantic, powerful bonds of kinship and shared culture remain in place. Those affinities of kith and kin now sit alongside the mutual economic interests that bind Ireland and the United States in the twenty-first century.

From what I have seen of Irish America, I expect its sense of Irishness to survive in the digital age. Indeed, the transformed universe of communications makes it easier than before to connect people and places across the Atlantic.

In almost four decades as a diplomat, I have learned to appreciate how the reach of Irish culture beyond our shores gives us an outsized international footprint. Interest in Irish history and literature is genuine and widespread. It is a boon for us to have so many scholars looking at our affairs from outside – it is a valuable antidote to the temptations of insularity.

We are fortunate indeed to have a number of centers of scholarship in the field of Irish Studies in the United States, among them Glucksman Ireland House at New York University. The quarter-century of the House's existence has coincided with remarkable changes across the Atlantic – in the early 1990s Northern Ireland remained a place of conflict while Ireland was still among the least-developed economies of Western Europe. Those changes have implications for the writers, scholars, artists, and students who cross Glucksman Ireland House's threshold every day.

I would argue that Ireland's standing in American eyes should no longer be anchored solely in the adversities of our past or in romantic versions of Ireland that are remote from contemporary realities. That being said, it is also true that the more traditional strands connecting our two countries will retain their importance and must never be neglected.

Finding a balance between the new realities and opportunities of the twenty-first century and the traditions of the past, near and distant, seems set to challenge students of Irish Studies in the decades to come.

Ireland's contemporary relationship with the United States connects two advanced, developed countries that share many values and interests. Economic ties are significant for both our countries ($100 billion in two-way trade, up to 100,000 Americans employed by Irish companies in all fifty states) and we have a shared stake in open societies and an inter-connected global economy that facilitates trade and investment.

Ireland now presents a diverse and confident face to the world. It has taken globalization fully in its stride and benefited significantly from its opportunities. Aside from the enduring appeal of its history and literature, Ireland's standing as a small, English-speaking country that has managed to combine a global outlook with the preservation of much of its traditional national character ought to make it an ongoing focus of scholarly attention.

Irishness in the twenty-first century is a global phenomenon that cannot be understood without reference to the various strands of Irish identity around the world. Prime among these is the story of Irish America, and it makes sense for us to come to terms with this particular expression of what it means to be Irish in today's world. Irish America is therefore deserving of serious attention, and it is good to see that Glucksman Ireland House has added this dimension to its field of activity.

Ireland's connections with America are likely to strengthen in the coming years as Britain departs the European Union. At that time, Ireland will be the EU's sole English-speaking country, making it well placed as a European base for American companies. Given our close historical and cultural connections with America through the American Irish, Ireland seems poised to play a bigger role as a conduit between the US and the EU. It seems to me that Irish people have an instinctively better understanding of America than many other Europeans.

As that process unfolds, Ireland will be marking a number of centenary milestones, culminating in 2022 in the 100th anniversary of our independent Irish State. The second century of Irish independence is bound to differ significantly from our first, in part because of Ireland's current level of social and economic advancement. The challenges we will face will have more in common with those of the United States than was the case a century ago, or at any time during the intervening years. That will require us to forge a new relationship with the United States and a new understanding of Irish America. As Eavan Boland has written, 'this time and now we need them.'

I expect NYU's Glucksman Ireland House to play a key role in exploring the new realities of Ireland and Irish America. As the House passes its quarter-century milestone, we should pay tribute to those who made this journey possible, notably Lew Glucksman and Loretta Brennan Glucksman for their generous support for Irish Studies.

I look back with pride at the generations of Irishmen and women who made the arduous journey across the Atlantic and at those who have created the more recent, mutually beneficial exchanges in business and in the professions. In addition to these potent human and commercial ties, I hope that the future will bring enhanced interaction in the realm of ideas and values. A dynamic flow of knowledge and creative energy back and forth across the Atlantic would be an apt way to build on a rich Irish-American heritage. It would help take our unique transatlantic partnership to a new and exciting level in the decades ahead.

Danial Mulhall is the Irish Ambassador to the United States.

Facing page, clockwise from top: Joyous students toss their hats in the air. Photo courtesy of James Higgins. NYU's Skirball Center was inaugurated in October 2003 with the sound and energy of Irish music and dance when Glucksman Ireland House celebrated the tenth anniversary with stellar talent such as that of Eileen Ivers. ©NYU. George Doherty, former board president, and and his wife Robbi enjoy the tenth-anniversary celebrations of Glucksman Ireland House. ©NYU.

# An Abundance
# of Stories

# GINA MARIE GUADAGNINO

Between the arrival of Patrick and the year 720, the Annals of Ulster records the names of fewer than ten women – although it is noted in the year 576 that there was 'a spark of leprosy and an unheard of abundance of nuts.' It has always struck me as remarkable that the annalists were observant enough to remark upon the country's nut yield, yet were not capable of recording the existence of more than ten women. Certainly, one supposes, there must have been more than ten women living in Ireland over the course of nearly three hundred years.

As a scholar, I obviously recognize how stringently sex-segregated medieval Irish society was, and understand that, as a result of European Christian religious and political power structures, the position of women and their ability to influence society were deeply constrained. Given that context, there is nothing unusual about the dearth of women in recorded medieval history, particularly in an account like the Annals of Ulster, which provides only the barest summary of each year. If this peculiar notation on the part of the annalists intrigues me, my path as scholar seems straightforward. I can delve into the primary texts of the period and compile a body of research that illuminates the environment in which the Annals were written. I can compare those texts to corroborating materials about the ways leprosy spread and was treated in the sixth century, and I can examine secondary sources, turning to dendrochronology or ice-core analysis, to examine the weather patterns that might have led to a nut crop so impressive that it demanded commentary in a document that otherwise confines itself to listing battles and the deaths of important men. I can pore through hagiography and draw suppositions about why St. Brigit was so revered that five of those mentions of women invoke her name; two entries suggesting her possible years of birth, and three entries listing contenders for the year of her death. I can draw conclusions from this broad, interdisciplinary corpus of research that will paint the most accurate possible picture of the world in which the annalists lived, providing insight as to the reasons behind their decisions regarding the types of events they chose to record.

But as a writer, I want to envision how extraordinary those women must have been to warrant mentioning, and use that research as a springboard to invent their stories. I could begin with the death of Mor Muman in 632, already mythologized in the tenth-century Book of Leinster. A sovereignty goddess under an enchantment, she is a fertile source for imagination. I can peel away the fantastical elements of her story and reveal the true woman, revered as Queen of Munster. And I can ask: who was Duinsech, wife of Domnall (who, while we're asking, was Domnall?), and why was her death in 639 sufficient fodder for the annalists' pens? Did she die young, in childbirth, remarked upon only because she was married to a powerful or notable man? Or did she die after a long and illustrious life of her own? As a writer of historical fiction, I have the ability to answer those questions, weaving the scholar's research into a rich tapestry in which Duinsech becomes more than a name inscribed on a calf-skin page. I can decide that she was, perhaps, a wealthy patroness of the arts, endowing the very scriptorium where the annalists painstakingly immortalized her in ink. And what

NYU Summer in Dublin, 2018: students and faculty meet the President of Ireland, Michael D. Higgins, at his historic home, Áras an Uachtaráin, in Dublin's Phoenix Park. © NYU.

of Coblaith, daughter of Canu, who died in 690? Her name, which means 'victorious sovereignty,' suggests a warrior queen, a figure from the Táin Bó Cúailnge come to life. I could write of her striding across the battlefield, a great ruler in her own right.

I can also decide what species of nut was so abundant – I'm partial to hazelnuts, myself.

To consider whether I came to write historical fiction because of my love of scholarship, or if I began to study history to further my creative writing, is to engage in something of a mental Mobius strip:

159

a perpetual loop in which the reason for one becomes the impetus for the other. Somehow, I cannot divorce the two. As an undergraduate at New York University, minoring in Irish Studies, I made the attempt, undertaking an independent study in which I catalogued the names of women listed in various editions of the Irish annals. It was in the basement lounge of Glucksman Ireland House, ubiquitous teacup in hand, that I first encountered the curious notations of 576 – a year in which, apparently, there were no women of significance, but Ireland's nut crop was uncommonly bountiful.

For reasons too convoluted and Byzantine to enumerate here, this enterprise, conducted under the tutelage of several professors at Glucksman Ireland House, ultimately commenced a chain of events that sent me on a post-graduation research odyssey from Donegal to Dublin, scrambling over the broken stones of Neolithic passage tombs on the western coast and paging through brittle parchments in the magnificent National Archives with white-gloved hands. These efforts, undertaken with the assumption that the resultant scholarship would lead to acceptance in a Celtic Studies PhD program on one side of the Atlantic, instead ended in my completion of an MFA in Creative Writing on the other. The temptation to transform my years of research into a fictional narrative proved too strong, and the resultant marriage (remarriage, if you'll permit me to extend my previous metaphor) of fact and fancy was a creative thesis rooted in scholarship, the provenance of which could be directly traced back to my undergraduate contemplation of leprosy and nuts.

What does one do with a list of women's names handed down through the centuries? What does one do when the voices of women exiled to the margins and footnotes of history begin to whisper, begging for their stories to be told? The Annals of Ireland become like trees waiting to be shaken, and I am here to collect the abundant harvest. Between the neatly inscribed lines of years, in the tumbled ruins of monuments, in the ashes of hearths long cold, there are lost stories ripe for reimagining.

I submitted the manuscript of my second novel on the same spring day that I submitted my application to Glucksman's master's program in Irish and Irish-American Studies. I will begin drafting my third novel by the time the fall semester starts.

The remarkable thing to me now is that I ever thought I had to choose between being a scholar or being a novelist. At this moment in my life, when I have seen my short stories on the Irish diaspora in print, when my first novel is about to be published, when, in order to continue the flow of research that so inspires me, I must redouble my scholastic efforts, the green door of Glucksman Ireland House has been swung wide in welcome. If you need me, I'll be in the basement lounge with my cup of tea. And perhaps a bowl of hazelnuts.

Gina Marie Guadagnino is an author of historical fiction and an MA candidate in Irish Studies at Glucksman Ireland House.

# Irish Spider

# BILLY COLLINS

It was well worth traveling this far
just to sit in a box of sunlight
by a window in a cottage

with a cup of steaming tea
and to watch an Irish spider waiting
at the center of his dewy web

pretending to be just any spider at all—
a spider without a nation—
but not fooling me for a minute.

# A Dream Fulfilled, A Need Addressed

## A Quarter-Century on, a House Becomes a Home

# TERRY GOLWAY

*The approximate date and exact circumstances have been forgotten but this much is certain: There was a crowd, a large, eager, excuse-me, pardon-me, crowd gathered in Glucksman Ireland House one night when the program was new. And it was hardly the first such crowd. It was simply the latest of many. Loretta Brennan Glucksman was there, in the middle of it all, and as she surveyed the room she turned to Robert Scally, the House's director, and expressed her amazement not only over this night but every other night like this since it opened its doors.*
*And Scally replied by quoting something his Irish-born mother would have said:*
*'Clearly, there was a need.'*
*Clearly.*

It started as a conversation among friends in the late 1980s: Lew Glucksman, a member of New York University's board, Loretta Glucksman, NYU Chancellor Jay Oliva and Mary Ellen Oliva. All four had an abiding interest in the university and in Ireland, although, as his colleagues on the NYU board were delighted to remind him, Lew hadn't

Left: Lew Glucksman and NYU President Jay Oliva, from the early days. ©NYU.
Right: Lew and Loretta. ©NYU.

a drop of Irish blood. It didn't matter. He had been in love with Ireland and Irish culture since visiting there as a young sailor in the US Navy during the Second World War.

It was Lew who noted that NYU had several programs focusing on the language and culture of several nationalities or groups. Why not Ireland?

Why not? Oliva, the bagpipes-playing, Irish-speaking son of an immigrant from Galway, invited the Glucksmans to join him and his wife on an expedition to Ireland to seek advice and input from university administrators and faculty there. Loretta would remember that the four of them were not entirely certain about what they wanted, or even what they had in mind. They were simply looking for ideas. 'The Irish universities rolled out the red carpet for us,' she recalled. 'They all were eager to help.'

They came back better informed and utterly convinced that they were onto something. Through her work with the American Ireland Fund, Loretta found what she was looking for – evidence of interest, of a need for a place where scholars, writers and musicians and artists from Ireland could mingle, converse, and present their works to a New York audience in an academic setting.

The idea began to take shape, helped in no small way by Oliva's appointment as NYU president-elect in late 1990. A site for the new endeavor was selected – two end units of a stretch of university-owned townhouses on Washington Mews. The site would be gutted and renovated so that it fronted Fifth Avenue, and, as originally envisioned, it would be home to a center for Irish Studies. Boston College already had such a program, founded in 1979, and the University of Notre Dame was on the verge of creating a similar program.

On May 20, 1991, the university formally announced the creation of Glucksman Ireland House at a luncheon for 200 people, including Taoiseach Charles Haughey. 'NYU has a special interest in Ireland – its language, literature, history and culture – which have long been part of our curriculum,' Oliva told an audience of prominent Irish Americans from the worlds of business, journalism, the arts, politics and law-enforcement, including, in the latter category, a prosecutor from the Manhattan district attorney's office named John F. Kennedy Jr. 'Many Americans, especially in New York City,' Oliva continued, 'can trace their ancestry back to Ireland and would welcome greater opportunity to study the culture and politics of the country of their origin.'

A year later, NYU's dean of faculty, Duncan Rice, met with Robert Scally, then a member of the university's History Department, and Denis Donoghue, who held the university's Henry James Chair of English and American Letters, to seek their help in developing serious academic programs for the new institution. Scally taught British history, but his parents were both Irish born and he was known to be working on a book about Famine-era Ireland. Donoghue, well, he was *Denis*

IRISH STUDIES FUND
GLUCKSMAN IRELAND HOUSE
NEW YORK UNIVERSITY

Renowned literary critic Denis Donoghue gave Glucksman Ireland House instant credibility and visibility from its earliest days. ©NYU.

*Donoghue*, native of County Carlow and one of the nation's most-distinguished literary critics. They agreed to organize a series of five lectures around campus to raise awareness of the program before the House opened its doors.

That meeting, however, produced a good deal more than a lecture series. It was a critical step forward – Scally and Donoghue would go on to become the first fulltime faculty members in residence at Glucksman Ireland House. Their expertise would help shape the program's identity as a center for the study of literature and history.

Literature, of course, was an obvious field of concentration. And the program had a significant head start thanks to the legacy of longtime faculty member David H. Greene, son of an Irish immigrant, former chairman of NYU's English Department, biographer of the playwright J.M. Synge, and the owner of an extensive library of rare Irish books as well as a collection of personal letters from Sean O'Casey. He eventually donated the books to Glucksman Ireland House and the letters to NYU, creating a one-of-a-kind resource for faculty and students alike.

Greene's passion for Irish culture and literature helped set the stage for what was to come. When Glucksman Ireland House opened its doors, Donoghue provided instant credibility and visibility through his connection to the program. In addition to his criticism in leading literary journals, Donoghue had written or edited books on W.B. Yeats, Jonathan Swift, and Emily Dickinson, among others, and had published a well-received memoir, *Warrenpoint*, just a few years earlier.

Irish literature, then, was assured of its proper place in the House's academic endeavors. History was another matter entirely. It would not be an exaggeration to say that in choosing to emphasize Irish history as well as Irish literature, Glucksman Ireland House made a bold, almost defiant, statement about the importance of a field that inspired neither a good deal of respect nor much interest among academic historians in the United States.

'Irish history simply wasn't taken very seriously,' Scally recalled. 'Irish history was something that the Clancy Brothers sang about. Unlike Irish literature, it was a topic not considered worthy of university study. Irish history was taught, if at all, as a branch of British history and not a particularly happy one.'

Scally was named as the program's founding director almost by accident, or at least that's how he tells the story. He happened to be working on a manuscript that became his ground-breaking book, *The End of Hidden Ireland*, and because of his research on the topic, he was teaching a course in Irish history. Otherwise, he taught English and European history. 'Both of my parents were from the west of Ireland, so everyone assumed that's why I was interested in Ireland,' Scally said. But it was all just coincidence. And for Glucksman Ireland House, it was all just good fortune.

Scally and Donoghue were among those who marched across Washington Square Park on April 26, 1993, the day the House was opened, and after the ceremonies were over and the dignitaries were gone, they settled into their offices and went about the task of turning Lew and Loretta Glucksman's vision into reality.

One image from those early days has remained with Loretta, and it involves Denis Donoghue, all six feet, seven inches of him. She occasionally watched him negotiating the House's small spaces and sharp angles as he climbed to his back corner office on the second floor. The office struggled to accommodate him, or perhaps it was the other way around. 'As he unfolded his legs and stood to greet you in his office, it was like watching a giraffe,' Loretta said.

There was no specific plan for the House beyond the general charge to build something that would showcase the depth and breadth of Irish culture within the context of a university setting. Dean Rice had told Scally that he thought the directorship would take up no more than a few hours a week. That modest conception of Scally's new position lasted no more than, well, a few hours, as it quickly became clear that Glucksman Ireland House would be more than a place for faculty to gather, or a congenial spot to host the occasional visiting writer or scholar from Ireland. It became, quite literally in a matter of a few months, a place where Irish and Irish-American writers and thinkers launched their books, read their poetry, shared their research, and offered their insights.

Within three years of its opening, Glucksman Ireland House welcomed Eavan Boland, Derek Mahon, Seamus Deane, Nuala Ní Dhomnhaill, Roddy Doyle, Paul Muldoon, and Mary Gordon, to name just a few. Pete Hamill spoke about his legendary career as a journalist and novelist. Peter Quinn and Colum McCann launched their first novels, while William Kennedy read from a work in progress, and Frank McCourt read from *Angela's Ashes*. A collection entitled *Ireland's Women: Writings Past and Present* was launched. Seamus Heaney delivered a lecture entitled 'Orpheus in Ireland' to mark the House's first anniversary, and if there were any doubts about the viability of Glucksman Ireland House at that point, they were put to rest after Heaney's remarkable lecture. There was a built-in audience for the House and its visitors, an audience whose size and passion none of its founders quite understood when the project moved from conversation to implementation.

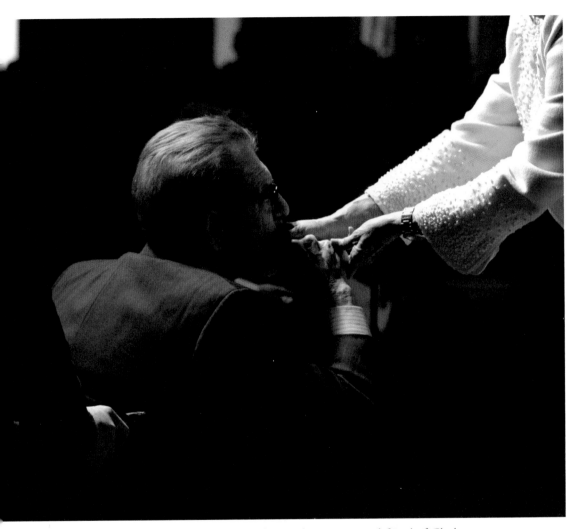

Pete Hamill, legendary journalist, novelist, teacher, mentor, and friend of Glucksman Ireland House, at the 2015 Gala. Photo courtesy of James Higgins.

'By the end of the first year, we were stunned by how many people in New York felt the need for something like Glucksman Ireland House,' Scally said. 'I don't think anybody realized how suddenly and quickly the place would grow.'

Seamus Heaney and Natasha Richardson were among the House's earliest supporters.

Both sides of the Atlantic immediately saw Glucksman Ireland House as a setting that was both academic and accessible. In its earliest years it even helped host Scannán, the first festival of Irish film to be screened in the city, no small feat in the pre-digital era.

The extent of its outsized influence at a young age became evident in late May, 1995, when scholars from around the world assembled under the House's leadership for an international conference on hunger to commemorate the 150th anniversary of the Great Hunger in Ireland. Mary Robinson, the President of Ireland, delivered the conference's keynote address, explicitly tying the historic suffering of mid-nineteenth-century Ireland to starvation in Africa and other parts of the developing world in the late twentieth century. She quoted from Scally's book about Famine-era Ballykilcline, County Roscommon, and then recalled the sights she saw during visits to several African countries. '[As] the head of state of a country which was once devastated by famine, I also felt the

NYU President Jay Oliva and Mary Robinson, president of Ireland, joined Robert Scally on stage at a milestone conference on hunger in 1995, which commemorated the 150th anniversary of the Famine. ©NYU.

terrible and helpless irony that this could actually be happening again,' she said.

Marion Casey, then a doctoral student at NYU, saw the hunger conference as a critical step forward for the House, both on and off campus. The university offered its full support to the event, Casey recalled, raising the House's profile for faculty and students alike. The conference also coincided with a successful, and controversial, effort to include the Famine in New York's school curriculum.

'This was the point when things began to shift radically at Glucksman Ireland House,' Casey said. 'The conference was high caliber, and it placed Ireland in a global conversation that is timeless.' Around the same time, Casey worked with the New Bedford Whaling Museum to display a tattered US flag in Glucksman Ireland House before its return to the National Museum of Ireland, where it had been donated by Clan na Gael in 1972. That flag flew from the mast of the whaling ship *Catalpa*

Writer Colm Tóibín and actor Fionnula Flanagan at a Glucksman Ireland House event. ©NYU.

in 1876, when it left Australia with several escaped Fenian prisoners on board. *Irish Times* journalist Sean Cronin recounted the dramatic episode, describing how the legendary Irish exile John Devoy organized the rescue not long after settling in New York City.

During those early years of the program, Scally impressed on the Glucksmans and others that the House ought to have a board to provide guidance as the program moved beyond its infancy. People like Barbara and Arthur Gelb, John Sharkey, and Carl Shanahan were among those who joined the board in those early years or who made phone calls to others in New York's Irish-American community. 'Everyone took their calls – they knew how to reach people,' recalled Loretta Brennan Glucksman. 'And as a result, we had a board of rock stars. And their involvement was critical. They provided a foundation for us, and it's why we lasted.' Founding staff member Patricia King also played a key role in outreach, for it seemed to Scally that she knew everybody 'both in Ireland and in North America.'

That network and the House's commitment to scholarship as well as public programming drew a succession of high-profile visiting scholars during those early years. They included Kevin Whelan, then with the Royal Irish Academy, Cormac O'Grada of University College Dublin, Jane Ohlmeyer of Trinity College Dublin, Kerby Miller from the University of Missouri-Columbia, Mary Hickman of London Metropolitan University, Clare Carroll of Queens College, Nicholas Canny of University College Galway, Luke Gibbons of Dublin City University, and Catherine McKenna of the City University of New York. The number of courses associated with the program grew from two, with an enrollment of thirty-four, in 1994–5 to ten, including three Irish language classes, in the spring of 1997, with an enrollment of 105.

The impressive lineup of visiting scholars and the growth in enrollment led NYU to approve an Irish Studies minor beginning in academic year 1996–7, just three years after the House opened its doors.

☘

New York University and Glucksman Ireland House hardly had a monopoly on Irish Studies on this side of the Atlantic. Boston College's program was well-established and Notre Dame's Donald and Marilyn Keough Program in Irish Studies, under the leadership of Seamus Deane, was born the same year as Glucksman Ireland House, 1993. Both programs emphasized the history, culture, and literature of Ireland, as did Glucksman Ireland House's academic offerings during its first few years.

Beginning in the late 1990s, however, the House took a turn on a road less traveled: The study of Irish America. It began in the spring of 1997 with the hiring of part-time faculty: Linda Dowling Almeida, who had just completed her doctorate in US History under the renowned NYU scholar of race and ethnicity, David M. Reimers, and Casey, who

Top: Renowned historian Richard White leads a discussion with graduate students in the House. ©NYU.

Bottom: Playwright John Patrick Shanley, with longtime Glucksman Ireland House faculty member Linda Dowling Almeida. ©NYU.

soon followed in fall 1998. Within five years, more than fifty students per class were enrolling each semester.

The fledgling exploration of Irish America received a boost from a new member of the board, Cormac O'Malley, son of the legendary Irish rebel and literary figure, Ernie O'Malley. 'We knew that Boston College and Notre Dame were concentrating on Irish studies, so we thought perhaps Irish America could be the place for us,' O'Malley recalled. He went on to advocate for a sharper focus on the intersection of Ireland with its diaspora in the United States.

The course selections were still tilted to the east, with offerings in Irish literature, the place of Ireland in early modern Europe, Irish women writers in the nineteenth century, and the history of Northern Ireland. But the scales began to tip west ever so slightly.

'Being in a city like New York, it seemed like a no-brainer to begin emphasizing the history and culture right outside the door,' Almeida said. 'Old Saint Patrick's Cathedral is just a couple of blocks away. The city could be a classroom for the study of Irish America.'

At around this time, the late 1990s, Marion Casey received a call from Dorothy Hayden Cudahy, a legend among the New York Irish who became, in 1989, the first woman to march up Fifth Avenue as the grand marshal of the New York St. Patrick's Day Parade. Cudahy had been host of a radio show, *Irish Memories*, for more than forty years and was the first American-born president of the Kilkenny Association. She was a one-person treasure trove of material for anyone who wished to know about the Irish in New York in the twentieth century.

Now, though, she was a widow who needed to downsize. She called Casey and told her she could have whatever was in the basement. Casey rounded up some friends and went to Cudahy's home with boxes. One of those boxes was filled with the papers of the American Irish Citizens Committee for the Re-Election of Mayor William O'Dwyer from 1949. All of it went into a rented storage space while Casey tried to figure out what to do next.

Not long thereafter, Anne Barrington, a longtime staff member at the Irish Consulate in New York, called Casey to see if perchance she might be interested in the consulate's collection of old newspapers, including a complete run of the *Irish People*, which was not in any library. Perchance, she was, and they, too, went into storage. Eventually, with the help of the archivist and social activist Debra Bernhardt at NYU's Tamiment Library and the then-Dean of NYU Libraries Carlton Rochelle, the Archives of Irish America was born in 1997, a signature achievement of Glucksman Ireland House and one that has elevated the program as a center for scholarly research.

Housed in NYU's Bobst Library, the collections in the Archives of Irish America have since grown to include more than 1,000 feet of records ranging from the papers of Judge James Comerford and Mick Moloney to the Irish Immigration Reform Movement and the Irish Repertory Theatre. The collections have also contributed to public history through online exhibits – especially '1981 Hunger Strikes: America Reacts' – and, in partnership with Culture Ireland and the New York Public Library for the Performing Arts in 2011, the 4,000-square-foot historical retrospective, 'The Ties that Bind: Performing Ireland, Becoming American.'

Another important research initiative, the Oral History of Irish America Project, launched in 2005. The project tells the story of life in the United States through the voices of Irish immigrants and their descendants. Students became a key part of the interview and preservation process, and thus a new pedagogical string was added to the Glucksman Ireland House bow. Its early success led to the hiring of oral historians Miriam Nyhan, Ide O'Carroll and Danielle Zach for specific theme-based collecting, so that today more than 350 oral histories are available for research.

'There's no other collection like it in the world,' Casey said. 'It is multi-generational, so it gives you a sense of what it means to be Irish over time, and it has given people an opportunity to talk about their lives and their work and their passion for their Irish-American identity.' The possibilities offered by digital technology also made it possible to share them well beyond the NYU campus through a series of podcasts over the last decade. Among the most poignant are *That Forever September Morning: Memories of 9/11*, *Reflections on a Political Life: Hugh Carey* and *Enjoying the Ride: The Irish in the NYC Horse and Carriage Industry, Then and Now*.

The House's emerging focus on Irish America took another step forward when board member Cormac O'Malley endowed an annual lecture named in honor of his father, Ernie O'Malley. Joe Lee, then a visiting professor at NYU, delivered the first Ernie O'Malley Lecture in December, 1999, noting that, 'like so many other Irish, several of my relatives are buried in America.' Nearly two decades later, the lecture has become one of the highlights of the academic year at Glucksman Ireland House. The major scholars in the field of Irish-American Studies have shared their work through this public forum, including Kerby Miller, Timothy Meagher, Charles Fanning, David Emmons, Janet Nolan, Kevin Kenny, Marion Casey and Francis Carroll. Shortly after Thomas Truxes spoke about 'Ireland, New York and the Eighteenth Century Atlantic World' in 2007, he joined the Glucksman Ireland House faculty and began directing the MA in World History for NYU's History Department.

All of this took place – perhaps by sheer coincidence, or perhaps not – during an extraordinary revival of interest in all things Irish in the United States. Books like Thomas Cahill's *How the Irish Saved Civilization*, Frank McCourt's *Angela's Ashes* and Alice McDermott's *Charming Billy* became bestsellers, not just for a week or two but for months. Barbara and Arthur Gelb published the first of three acclaimed biographical volumes on the great Irish-American playwright Eugene O'Neill. *Riverdance* became a Broadway sensation (and its star, Jean Butler, would eventually find a home at Glucksman Ireland House as an adjunct professor), as did Irish plays, from *The Beauty Queen of Leenane* to *The Steward of Christendom* and many others, on and off Broadway. Irish movies moved from cultural curiosities to regular fare in American multiplexes.

The effect on the House was palpable, in part because some of those who were driving this Gaelic Revival in New York were friends of the program. Even as Frank McCourt traveled the world as Irish America's newest literary celebrity, he remained a frequent guest at the House, reading, introducing other writers, and supporting other events. 'Frank spent a lot of time with us, and he went from being known in a small Irish circle to becoming somebody everybody knew,' Scally recalled. 'And everything I asked him to do after *Angela's Ashes*, he did, and he did it with pleasure.'

'The timing for all of this could not have been better,' Loretta Brennan Glucksman said. 'We came along and then there was this explosion of interest in Ireland and in Irish America. History helped set the stage for us.'

Irish history, as hundreds of NYU students were learning through the House's dozen or so classes, has never lacked for drama, but at this moment in the late twentieth century, its principal actors were speaking lines never heard before, their roles rewritten, the plot line leading to unexpected places.

The long conflict in the north of Ireland, into which Irish America inevitably had been drawn, was coming to an end in the late 1990s. Onetime antagonists became partners for peace, still wary of each other to be sure, but nevertheless willing to take a chance on hope. In the middle of it all, quite literally, was a man from America named George Mitchell, a onetime US senator from Maine who served as President Bill Clinton's special envoy to Northern Ireland beginning in 1995. In another age, before history revised the script in Ireland, mediating the conflict in the north might have been described as a thankless task. But on November 2, 1998, just a few months after negotiating the Good Friday Agreement, George Mitchell earned a rousing ovation

George Mitchell, pausing here for a selfie, launched his book, *The Negotiator*, at the House. Photo courtesy of James Higgins.

as the guest of honor at Glucksman Ireland House's celebration of its fifth anniversary. He would later be awarded the Presidential Medal of Freedom for his efforts, and his patience, integrity, and quiet competence were chronicled in fictional form by Colum McCann in his brilliant 2013 novel, *Transatlantic*. Mitchell later launched his own book, *The Negotiator*, at the House in 2015.

'George Mitchell,' Loretta Brennan Glucksman said years later, 'made it possible for all of us to want to work together. We as a community are stronger because of him.'

❖

As the century turned there were five full-time faculty members and three visiting or adjunct instructors associated with Glucksman Ireland House. The program offered twenty-seven courses to nearly 800 students during the 2000-2001 academic year. In their annual report to the House's board, Scally and O'Malley, now the president of the board of advisors, noted simply that when the program began there were two undergraduate classes and ten students.

The program's growth and energy were reflected not simply in the number of students but in their enthusiasm. They formed two new organizations, the Glucksman Ireland House Undergraduate Student Association and Grian (Irish for 'sun'), a multi-university Irish studies graduate group based at the House and designed to encourage and support emerging scholars in the New York area. Grian sponsored several conferences on Irish studies and published five issues of the annual interdisciplinary journal *Foilsiú*.

The new century also saw the debut of *Radharc: Chronicles of Glucksman Ireland House*. This annual journal printed lectures presented at the House exploring culture, politics, identity and literature in Ireland and Irish America. Eventually *Radharc* would be reimagined and rebranded as the *American Journal of Irish Studies* in 2012. It includes transcripts of the House's three named lectures, The Ernie O'Malley Lecture, focused on Irish-American topics, the Irish Institute of New York Lecture, which examines a contemporary Irish subject, and the Barra O Donnabhain Lecture, conducted in the Irish language and named in honor of the respected Irish language columnist for the *Irish Echo*.

A decade had passed since President Oliva's announcement of this new creation called Glucksman Ireland House. Founding director Bob Scally decided it was time to turn the program over to new leadership after presiding over growth and successes nobody had anticipated and yet now seemed entirely inevitable. (Scally continued to teach until his full retirement in 2006.)

The House's new director was no stranger to the place, and certainly no stranger to anyone who was conversant in Irish historiography. J. Joseph Lee had made his mark in Ireland as a professor of history at University College Cork and as the author of two seminal books, *Ireland 1912–1985: Politics and Society* and *The Modernisation of Irish Society, 1848–1918*. He spent several years as a member of Seanad Éireann, the Irish Senate, where he campaigned for a university reform bill – 'the only way to get change accomplished,' he later recalled, 'is to be in a position to embarrass the people who were trying to stop it.' He left the Seanad after four years, having accomplished the task through the means he described.

Professor Joe Lee leads a history graduate seminar. In the background is a bust of author Mary Lavin by Helen Huntington Hooker. ©NYU.

As Glucksman Ireland House's new director, Lee saw his task as relatively straightforward: 'All I had to do,' he said, 'is not knock down the achievements made under Bob Scally.'

It was a modest goal – far too modest, as events would show.

The House's public programs continued to attract well-known scholars, writers, poets, musicians and artists from Ireland and Irish America, and they invariably found themselves speaking to standing-room only audiences. They streamed in from Fifth Avenue every Thursday night for academic lectures, book launches, poetry readings and panel discussions.

Cormac O Grada spoke about 'Leopold Bloom and Irish Jewry,' Marianne Elliot discussed the historiography of Robert Emmet, music historian David Kincaid launched an album of songs from the American Civil War, and Monsignor Thomas Shelley explained the Archdiocese of New York's Hibernarchy. Lucy McDiarmid launched *The Irish Art of Controversy*. The Abbey Theatre performed J.M. Synge's *Playboy of the Western World* at the Skirball Center, and the House celebrated the career of journalist Jimmy Breslin. A series entitled 'The Irish on the Americans' in 2004 brought Eavan Boland for a discussion of the work of Edna St. Vincent Millay. Two Pulitzer Prize winners, Paul Muldoon and Billy Collins, read from their poetry. John Patrick Shanley talked about his Irish-American roots not long after his play, *Doubt*, opened on Broadway. Mary Higgins Clark, Edna O'Brien and Nuala O'Faolain read from their books.

'Hidden Truths: Bloody Sunday 1972' marked the thirtieth anniversary of this seminal event with a panel discussion among Martin McGuinness, Richard Harvey, Mary Hickman, Peter Pringle and Trisha Ziff. Jeffrey Sachs and George Soros delivered the first of two lectures in memory of the late US senator from New York, Daniel Patrick Moynihan. Denis Donoghue introduced his daughter Emma's short story collection, *The Woman Who Gave Birth to Rabbits*. And Glucksman Ireland House marked its tenth anniversary with 'West Along the Road,'

NYU distinguished professor Mick Moloney brings Irish culture around the world through his music. ©NYU.

a concert, recital series and conference organized by Mick Moloney, the new Global Distinguished Professor of Music and Irish Studies at NYU.

In 2007 the Irish Institute of New York endowed a new annual lecture series to focus on contemporary issues in Ireland, with the Rev. Dr. Diarmuid Martin, the Archbishop of Dublin, serving as the inaugural speaker. Following in his footsteps came Rev. John Dunlop, Bill Whelan, Garry Hynes, Frank McDonald, Margaret MacCurtain, Cathal Mac Coille, Darina Allen, Stephen Ferguson, and Sister Stanislaus Kennedy.

The Blarney Star concert series found a new home in Glucksman Ireland House and became a regular on the calendar, curated once a month on a Friday night by Don Meade, who ensured that the intimacy of 1 Washington Mews showcased the Atlantic world's finest Irish traditional musicians in a modern *seisiún*.

The program's continued emphasis on Irish-American history and culture led to the publication of *Making the Irish American: History and*

The Irish language is a key component of the House's undergraduate and graduate programs. Here, longtime Irish-language instructor Pádraig Ó Cearúill leads a class. ©NYU.

*Heritage of the Irish in the United States*, edited by Joe Lee and Marion Casey and published by NYU Press in 2006. In addition to essays by scholars such as Irene Whelan, Mary Corcoran and Rebecca Miller, it included reflections from Daniel Patrick Moynihan, Pete Hamill, Calvin Trillin, and Peter Quinn. The book, the editors wrote, was in part an attempt to compile new thinking – and some older insights – on Irish America since the unexpected revival of the 1990s.

That same year, 2006, the program achieved another milestone when the university approved a new graduate program. The unique MA in Irish and Irish-American Studies curriculum required an introductory interdisciplinary seminar taught by John Waters and a class on the Irish language and culture taught by Senior Irish Language lecturer Pádraig Ó Cearúill. Lee saw the graduate program as 'one of the program's biggest innovations,' in part because eventually it would attract a new cohort of students – older, non-traditional, and immensely eager. Those students, traditional and non-traditional alike, brought even more energy to the House and soon began producing new, original research guided by the House's faculty.

It would seem fair to say that Lew Glucksman could have never imagined that an off-handed remark to Jay Oliva back in the late 1980s – why not create a home for Irish studies at NYU? – could or would lead to all of this. A graduate program. New research and writing. Archives of international importance. A dozen undergraduate classes or more running in any given semester. Lectures, readings and performances on an almost weekly basis. Large, engaged audiences.

Then again, perhaps he knew it was bound to happen, for he had a keen and very personal appreciation for the enduring power and attraction of Irish culture and history. In any case, whether he anticipated the House's growth or not, he bore witness to the program's rapid maturation into a world-class academic institution and was its foremost champion.

Lew became ill and died at his home in Cobh on July 5, 2006 at the age of 80. Several years earlier, while presenting Lew with an honorary degree at University College Cork, Joe Lee paid tribute to the 'fusion of intellect and imagination, of thought and action, that has inspired Lew Glucksman to visualize a future of rapid change that is nonetheless rooted in, rather than reneging on, a cultural heritage beyond price.'

Through his generosity, his vision, his intellect and imagination, Lew Glucksman created a space to examine, interrogate, celebrate, revise, and above all preserve the cultural heritage of Ireland and Irish America in the heart of New York City. His memory is kept alive in many ways, not least of which is the annual presentation of the Lewis L. Glucksman Award for leadership to a member of the Irish-American business community.

♣

Clockwise from top left:
Liam Clancy performed at Glucksman Ireland House not long before he died in 2009.

Joannie Madden, founder of Cherish the Ladies, entertains guests at the House's annual gala in 2015. Photo courtesy of James Higgins.

Songwriter, vocalist, and actor Glen Hansard, performing at the House. ©NYU and Stacy Libokmeto.

Glucksman Ireland House continued to find innovative and challenging ways to connect Ireland and America through history, literature, and public programs, and, what's more, to examine Irish culture in a broader, global perspective. It played host to Dana Lyn and Tina Lech, two women Asian-American fiddlers, who performed Irish music as part of the Blarney Star concert series. Two of the House's professors, Marion Casey and John Waters, led a discussion of a short film, *We Live in Ireland*, about Chinese immigrants in Ireland. The first American to win a senior all-Ireland championship in fiddling, Kathleen Collins, performed selections from a new album. Enniscorthy-born Colm Tóibín launched his new novel, *Brooklyn*, and the Kerry-born historian Joe Lee reflected on the life and career of the New York statesman Daniel Patrick Moynihan.

Shortly before he died in 2009, Liam Clancy came by the House to perform one more time, to tell a few more stories. He was the last member of the four performers – the Clancy Brothers and Tommy Makem – who created such a sensation in the 1960s, reviving Irish folk music on both sides of the Atlantic. Clancy was ill at the time, and those who were privileged to be on hand sensed that they were witnessing the end of an era.

The House added yet another new annual event in 2011 with the Tom Quinlan Lecture in Poetry, a gift from Glucksman Ireland House board member Joe Quinlan to honor his father, a teacher and lover of poetry. Seamus Heaney delivered the inaugural lecture with the event's namesake in the audience. Heaney returned to Glucksman Ireland House in 2013 for a gala dinner to mark its twentieth anniversary. He read from a poem composed in honor of the evening's honoree, Loretta Brennan Glucksman:

The edifice off 1 Fifth Avenue
Fit monument to herself and Lew –
Is like a small translated Clonmacnoise,
An amplifier for the native voice.

Clockwise from top:
Two men from the north: Liam Neeson and Seamus Heaney. ©NYU.

Ted Smyth, businessman and former diplomat, assumed the presidency of the Advisory Board in the summer of 2018.

Irish Ambassador Anne Anderson with NYU President Andrew Hamilton. ©NYU.

It was Seamus Heaney's final visit to the House and to New York. He died six months later, on August, 30, 2013.

It was clear, as the House looked back at its first twenty years and ahead to the next twenty, that its programs, speakers, scholarship and artistry deserved a wider audience. With that in mind, the *Glucksman Ireland House Radio Hour*, hosted by Miriam Nyhan Grey, was launched on Saturday mornings preceding a fixture of Irish-American radio, the *Adrian Flannelly Show*. Nyhan's program has included live interviews as well as recordings of lectures at the House, and has succeeded in extending its reach to the general public and to potential students.

The second decade of the twenty-first century brought yet another burst of activity and energy at Glucksman House Ireland as Ireland and Irish America prepared for a decade of commemorations coinciding with the centennials of the Dublin Lockout, the start of the First World War, the Easter Rising, the Irish War of Independence, the founding of the Irish Free State, and the Irish Civil War. Early on in the process, Glucksman Ireland House formed a special subcommittee to plan a series of programs focused on Irish America's role in the Rising. The result was an extraordinary effort that commemorated the Rising's anniversary with quiet dignity, fresh inquiry, and scholarly reflection. The highlight of the programming was a two-day conference in downtown Manhattan that brought established scholars and several graduate students from the Glucksman Ireland House program together to hear new research and about the Irish men and women in America who organized and supported the Rising. A day after the conference, Glucksman Ireland House board member Peter Quinn delivered a remarkable address on behalf of the city's Irish-American community for the Irish Government's American commemoration.

Many of the papers presented at the conference were accepted for publication in a book entitled *Ireland's Allies: America and the 1916 Easter Rising*, published by University College Dublin Press. The inclusion in the book of several papers by Glucksman Ireland House

Inaugurating the Tom Quinlan Lecture in Poetry, Loretta Brennan Glucksman, Tom Quinlan, Seamus Heaney and board member Joe Quinlan, who endowed the lecture in honor of his father. ©NYU.

graduate students was a testament to the high level of research being undertaken in the program, and the equally high level of guidance offered by Glucksman Ireland House faculty.

As the House began its own season of commemoration to mark its twenty-fifth anniversary, another transition was underway. Joe Lee retired as director in September, 2017, after fifteen memorable years. The renowned scholar of the Jewish experience in America, Hasia R. Diner, was named as interim director. Diner was no stranger to research on Ireland and the Irish. Her publications include *Erin's Daughters in America: Irish Immigrant Women in the Nineteenth Century* and *Hungering for America: Italian, Irish, and Jewish Foodways in the Age of Migration.*

Former interim director Hasia Diner, center, with, from left, Loretta Brennan Glucksman, Miriam Nyhan Grey, former board president Judith McGuire and longtime board member Patricia Harty. Photo courtesy of James Higgins.

In the fall of 2018, the renowned historian Kevin Kenny was named director of Glucksman Ireland House. Before coming to New York, Kenny spent many years at Boston College, where he chaired the History Department.

In the meantime, Judith McGuire retired as chair of the House's board and was replaced by Ted Smyth, a former Irish diplomat and longtime board member. 'I'm honored to become the board's president,' Smyth said, 'and I'm grateful to my predecessors, Judith McGuire, George Doherty and Cormac O'Malley. I'm looking forward to working with my fellow board members, all of whom are passionately committed to Irish and Irish-American Studies.'

Above: The House's first two directors, Bob Scally and Joe Lee, with longtime board member and former board president Cormac O'Malley and Consul General Ciarán Madden.
Photo courtesy of Nuala Purcell.

Left: Kevin Kenny was appointed director of Glucksman Ireland House in fall 2018. Photo courtesy of Kevin Kenny.

Facing page:
Taoiseach Leo Varadkar with the grand marshal of the 2018 St. Patrick's Day parade in New York, Loretta Brennan Glucksman. Photo courtesy of James Higgins.

Hundreds gathered to celebrate the twenty-fifth anniversary at Glucksman Ireland House's annual gala in late February, 2018, as Paul Muldoon received the House's annual Seamus Heaney Award for Arts and Letters from the poet's widow, Marie Heaney, and Carl Shanahan was presented with the Lewis L. Glucksman Award for Leadership.

And just a few weeks later, the co-founder of Glucksman Ireland House led a bit of a march through the streets of New York. It was slightly larger than the march across Washington Square Park in 1993 – larger by a few thousand marchers and a few million spectators. As the grand marshal of the New York St. Patrick's Day Parade, Loretta Brennan Glucksman, philanthropist, muse and advocate, only the fifth woman in the parade's centuries-long history, was presented with the thanks and applause of a community that had been waiting for something like Glucksman Ireland House for many years.

It was all so very clear.

# Tribute to
# Lew Glucksman

# J.J. LEE

*A Sheansailéir, a Árd Mhaor agus a mhuintir na hOllscoile*
*Cuis áthais dom Lewis L. Glucksman a chur in aithne dibh, agus muid ag*
*ceiliuradh bronnadh na céime onórai seo air inniu.*

'We had the experience but missed the meaning,' mused T.S. Eliot. Lew Glucksman has always drawn meaning from his experience. A striking unity emerges from even so diverse a range of activity, a pattern of action informed by thought, and of thought honed and disciplined by immersion in the crucible of action.

The love of the sea, acquired from life in the U.S. navy during and after the Second World War, translated into service as a Commissioner of the Port Authority of New York and New Jersey, one of the largest public institutions in the United States, into support too for the Virginia Institute of Maritime Studies, and for the capaciously conceived Map Library of Trinity College Dublin.

His redoubtable record in the world of high finance, whether in chairing his own investment bank, or as Chairman or President or CEO, and regularly a Finance and Audit Committee member, in firms as renowned as Lehman Brothers, Smith Barney, Revlon, and many others, has earned him a legendary reputation on Wall Street, translating in turn into service to his *almae matres*, as a member of the Board of Visitors of the College of William and Mary, the Board of Trustees and Finance Committee of New York University, Professor of Finance in the Graduate Business School of NYU, and member of the Advisory Board of Ireland's National Treasury Management Agency at the invitation of the then Minister for Finance, Bertie Ahern.

A man of the boat, and a man of the Bourse, then, but above all, a man of the book – with a love of culture in general, and literature in particular, that led him to Ireland, translating into the Glucksman Chair for Literature; the Glucksman Reading Room; and a funding drive for the Library, at the University of Limerick: translating further into support for the new Millennium Wing of the National Gallery.

Translating, too, into Glucksman Ireland House of New York University. I had just begun thinking about this address when I happened to be watching a program on *Teilifís na Gaeilge* about a Brooklyn-based artist, Elizabeth O'Reilly, born in Cork. Up on the screen came that well-loved House, just before Fifth Avenue issues into Washington Square, with the lens zooming in on the plaque that reads Lewis L. and Loretta Brennan Glucksman Ireland House, for it is a joint creation of himself and Loretta, his wife, support, and partner extraordinaire, herself tireless in philanthropic endeavor for Irish culture, not least as Chair of the American Ireland Fund.

Glucksman Ireland House featured in that program because Elizabeth O'Reilly felt a need to rediscover the language she had lost, and she turned to the Irish classes in Glucksman Ireland House, which, incidentally, are regularly oversubscribed. Irish language courses are but one feature of a cultural milieu that has become, within a decade, a conduit for the best of Irish culture, North and South, to flow into the American mainstream, and for the best of American culture, in all its exuberant ethnic variety, to enrich in turn an Irish culture that has the confidence and composure to welcome all, to learn from all, but to yield to none, blending scholarship with style, and energy with elegance, in the gracious ambience of Glucksman Ireland House.

The historian, without seeking to simplify a complex historical record, may perceive in the joining together in the very name of Glucksman Ireland House a felicitous association of two highly creative immigrant peoples to America, in both of whom, making appropriate allowance for rhetorical romanticisation, a love of learning had survived even their darkest days, and both of whom too came with ample cause to know their genealogy, an association of names moreover that now resonates in universities from Cork to Jerusalem.

The very idea of the university itself is nowadays, of course, a subject of intense debate. Central to that debate is the relation between business and the university. We have much to learn from that fusion of intellect and imagination, of thought and action, that has inspired Lew Glucksman to visualize a future of rapid change that is nonetheless rooted in, rather than reneging on, a cultural heritage beyond price.

Lew Glucksman has touched nothing to which he hasn't made a difference. A steadfast man, he knows who he is and he does it his way. Happily, Ireland is a large part of that way. Now that he has come to live in Cork, in the process refurbishing, indeed rejuvenating, a great house and garden, we can welcome him as an honorary Corkman.

For if he has already put us in his debt by accepting the Chair of the Cork University Foundation Board, whose role is so crucial to the future of the university, and thus of Cork itself, he comes bearing no greater gift than the presence of Loretta and himself amongst us.

*A Sheansailéir, nil sé ar mo chumas, agus mé ag druidim chun deiridh, ach blas beag bideach a thabhairt dén mhéid ata déanta ag an bhfear seo chun saol cultúrtha agus saol intleachtúla na hÉireann a chothu, i bhfus agus i gcéin.*

For his use of his own talents, and for having opened so many doors for so many others to develop their talents in the world of learning, it

Lew Glucksman and Joe Lee in 2002, when Lew received an honorary doctor of laws degree from the National University of Ireland. ©NYU.

is an honor to present Lewis L. Glucksman to the Chancellor of the National University of Ireland for the conferring of the degree of Doctor of Laws, *honoris causa.*

*Praehonorabilis Cancellarie, Totaque Universitas: Praesento vobis, hunc meum filium, quem scio tam moribus, quam doctrina habilem et idoneum esse qui admittatur, honoris causa, ad gradum Doctoratus in utroque Jure, tam Civili quam Canonico, idque tibi fide mea testur ac spondeo, totique Academ iae.*

Delivered by Professor J.J. Lee on 11 May 2002 in University College Cork on the occasion of the conferring of the degree of Doctor of Laws, *honoris causa,* on Lewis L. Glucksman.

# Lauds For Loretta

# SEAMUS HEANEY

How can we laud her? Let me count the ways.
Her ready smile, serene attentive gaze,
Her hostess role on both sides of the ocean,
Her work for peace when the land was in commotion.
Philanthropy, unstinted, open-handed,
Requests for help from every quarter granted,
Benefactor, with her mighty spouse,
Of galleries, colleges and Ireland House.
That edifice off 1 Fifth Avenue –
Fit monument to herself and Lew –
Is like a small translated Clonmacnoise,
An amplifier for the native voice
Of Irish writing, culture, scholarship,
An answer given to the famine ship,
A feis, a court of poetry, a seisiún,
Academy and legacy, a boon.
Twenty years ago, a kilted piper,
The Taoiseach, Albert Reynolds, at his heel,
Led a starry crowd across the Square:
Jay Oliva, James Galway, Brian Friel,

Loretta, Lew himself, the whole aosdána,
With supporting cast, O'Shea, Cusack, O'Hara.
That April day, a mark was made in time
As we processed in step like words in rhyme,
As dúchas met diaspora and combined
Indomitable Irishry of mind
With the Big Apple of Knowledge: thus we set a
Crown upon the labours of Loretta
And great Lew, while Cathleen Ní Houlihan
Looked down upon this Lass of Allentown
And recognized her as an aisling geal,
A presence, guardian spirit, and a pal.
'She is foremost of those that I would hear praised'
Said Yeats of Maud, but for us LBG
Is she to whom all glasses must be raised,
So rise up now and toast our honouree.

Seamus Heaney won the Nobel Prize for Literature in 1995.